Indian Rock Paintings
of the Great Lakes

The Agawa Site, Lake Superior,

Near Devil's Bay, Lake of the Woods

INDIAN
ROCK PAINTINGS
OF THE
GREAT LAKES

Second Edition

By Selwyn Dewdney and
Kenneth E. Kidd

PUBLISHED FOR THE QUETICO FOUNDATION
BY UNIVERSITY OF TORONTO PRESS

Quetico Foundation Series

1. THE INDIANS OF QUETICO. By E. S. Coatsworth
2. QUETICO GEOLOGY. By V. B. Meen
3. CANOE TRAILS THROUGH QUETICO. By Keith Denis
4. INDIAN ROCK PAINTINGS OF THE GREAT LAKES. By
   Selwyn Dewdney and Kenneth E. Kidd

The authors gratefully acknowledge the generous
assistance and advice of many individuals and organiza-
tions on which the years of extensive field work were so
dependent. The Quetico Foundation is greatly indebted
to the Government of Ontario for its financial assistance
in the publication of this book.

Foreword

WHEN ASKED to support the publication of *Indian Rock Paintings of the Great Lakes* and, in October 1961, to contribute the Foreword, I did so with considerable enthusiasm. The permanent recording of these interesting and exciting pictographs was an important event of historic significance. That the original edition is now out of print is a tribute to all those who made its publication possible.

My remarks in the Foreword of 1961 continue to be appropriate so I am repeating them in essence below.

Fortunately, the Quetico Foundation, with the essential assistance of the Royal Ontario Museum and departments of the Government of Ontario, re-engaged Mr. Selwyn Dewdney to collect evidence of further "rock painting" sites, visit them and make further recordings. This second edition affirms the success of his additional efforts.

This edition contains new drawings and new descriptive material, so that all told this second edition gives a most comprehensive pictorial description of pictographs appearing throughout Ontario.

Mr. Kenneth E. Kidd who is now Associate Professor of Anthropology, Trent University, Peterborough, Ontario, has again reviewed Mr. Dewdney's text and has also supplied an Epilogue to his original "Anthropological Background."

It is indeed a pleasure again to endorse particularly the research and educational efforts of the Quetico Foundation. Their primary interest is in wilderness parks for recreational and scientific purposes. It is stimulating to see an important group of businessmen and scholars joining together to promote a better understanding of the vital and salutary benefits derived from union with nature. The preservation of sufficient areas in their primitive state becomes more and more important to our citizens as the proportion of urban population continues to swell.

Lindsay, Ontario
January 1967

LESLIE M. FROST

Original Foreword

THIS BOOK is the outcome of an exciting and challenging quest by Mr. Selwyn Dewdney, artist and author, and Mr. Kenneth E. Kidd, Curator, Department of Ethnology, Royal Ontario Museum, to discover and record the Indian rock paintings, or pictographs as they are now called, of Northern Ontario. These pictographs, which may be found on the rock faces along the waterways of the Canadian Shield from Lake Mazinaw, north of Belleville, to the Ontario-Manitoba boundary, provide evidence of the cultural achievements of the early inhabitants of our Province. No doubt, the small symbols aroused the speculative interest and curiosity of the early voyageurs and others who have followed them. But it is only today, through the efforts of the authors of this volume, as well as the Quetico Foundation, the Royal Ontario Museum, and the Departments of the Government of Ontario, that they are being presented to a wider audience.

A large number of pictographs are to be found within Quetico Park's 1,750 square miles. In order better to assure the preservation of this natural wilderness, it was my privilege two years ago, along with the President of the United States, to establish a Committee consisting of residents of both Ontario and of the United States. The Committee is making a notable contribution to the establishment of a co-ordinated development plan for the Quetico-Superior Area on both sides of the international border. The Quetico Foundation materially assisted in fostering the establishment of this Committee.

In addition to this work, the Quetico Foundation has been engaged in a variety of studies and educational projects. This volume is the fourth in the series that has been published. The Government of Ontario is pleased to have been associated with the Foundation and the Royal Ontario Museum in this work. The publication of this volume should help to quicken interest in our early history and stimulate further research and study.

LESLIE M. FROST
Prime Minister of Ontario

Lindsay, Ontario
October 18, 1961

vi

Contents

Preface to the Second Edition

THE FIRST EDITION of this book came off the press in 1962. Since then I have recorded another sixty-three occurrences of aboriginal rock art in Ontario and adjacent Minnesota, bringing the total to one hundred and sixty-six. The title is now something of a misnomer, for the region covered in the revised book extends far beyond the Great Lakes drainage. The reader should keep in mind, too, that there are scores of related sites in northern Manitoba and Saskatchewan.

Most of the new material in this revised edition will be found under "The Search Continued," but I have also appended some "Further thoughts" to the section, "The Aboriginal Artist." Additional illustrations include four quadricolours and a distribution map. To provide useful site locations would have involved the expense of an extra forty pages, for the omission of which we can only offer our regrets.

Some readers of the first edition have misunderstood the fragmentary nature of many of the small marginal drawings and assumed the printers were at fault. In fact, they faithfully reproduced my original drawings, which are as close to the actual appearance of the paintings, *in situ,* as I could achieve within the limitations of pen and ink renderings. To have included only those paintings that were unimpaired by weathering or lichen encroachment would have created a false impression of the originals. On the other hand, I have been alert to the copyist's constant temptation to project his own images into the definition of amorphous passages.

I take some satisfaction in the knowledge that the systematic field recording programme, initiated by Kenneth E. Kidd in 1957, has been the first of its scope on this continent. Elsewhere, however, such work now proceeds apace on every continent, and publications multiply around the globe with each passing year. This emerging interest is not merely a matter of aesthetics. Rather it is part of a renewed, world-wide urge to examine our human origins. For here lie substantial clues to what man was, and therefore is. Here are found the first preliterate gropings toward the written word. Here, too, we may look for light on the time-shadowed origins of man's ancient need to express through visual imagery the yearnings that lie beyond—or beneath—the reach of words.

SELWYN DEWDNEY, 1967

Editorial Note

The current standardized spelling of the word "Ojibwa," traditionally pronounced and frequently still spelled Ojib*way*, illustrates the confusion over the rendering of aboriginal Indian words for English-speaking readers. Chippewa, Chippeway, and Otchipwé are other variants of the same word. The following key to pronunciation of Ojibwa(y) words appearing in the text was devised by a trained linguist, Mrs. Jean H. Rogers, and is based on her study of the language as spoken by a northern band of Ojibwa at Round Lake. As she warns: "This key is an attempt to give the closest equivalents to Ojibwa sounds that exist in English. It is not phonetically accurate, but the best that can be done within the limitations of English sounds and English spelling."

KEY

Vowels			Consonants		
	ey	as in "key"		ch	as in "chin"
	ay	as in "say"		sh	as in "she"
	ow	as in "bowl"		zh	as in "azure"
	iw	as in "ewe"		z	as in "buzz"
	i	as in "pin"		h	as in "hill"
	u	as in "cut"			(before a consonant *h*
					sounds like the *ch* in
					"loch" or in the German "nacht")

Each Ojibwa word, on its first appearance in the text, is italicized, and hyphenated to avoid confusion between the syllables. Thereafter it is treated as a familiar word.

Illustrations

All the drawings reproduced in red, with the exception of the McInnes drawing on page 72 and the Agawa deer on page 83, are drawn to the scale of one inch to the foot, making them one twelfth actual size. An attempt has been made to indicate the relative strength of the painting by heavy or light shading, though the faintest have been exaggerated for visibility's sake. The reproduced photographs of water colours from the Museum collection are also, for the most part, greatly reduced in scale, but not consistently. Readers interested in the actual size of the originals will find in most cases that adjacent line drawings in red provide the needed clue. Other photographs including the eight quadricolours, unless designated otherwise, were taken by Selwyn Dewdney.

The Quest

How It Began

About fifteen miles southeast of Kenora, in the water labyrinth of channels, bays, and islands so typical of Lake of the Woods, you will come to the outlet of Blindfold Lake. Nearby, on the north shore, is a vertical rock above a sloping ledge, its face scattered with Indian paintings. As a boy I knew the place. Yet I gave the pictures only a glance, being far more fascinated by the offerings on the ledge, remnants of rotted clothing, chipped and rusted enamelware, and traces of tobacco.

Fifteen years later and 400 miles farther east I ran across other Indian paintings on the Fairy Point rocks of Lake Missinaibi. Later, revisiting the place with my wife, I made quick sketches of a few of the symbols—depressingly inaccurate ones, I was to learn years later. Yet over all the years that I knew of these two sites it never occurred to me that there might be others.

In 1955, as a book illustrator in search of fresh source material on the costume of early Indians in Canada, I called on Kenneth E. Kidd, Curator

2

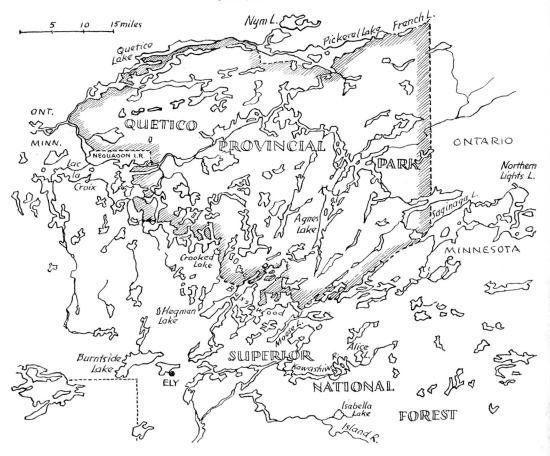

of Ethnology at the Royal Ontario Museum. Recognizing each other as acquaintances from college days, we lunched together.

Only that summer Ken had viewed the impressive Lac la Croix paintings in Quetico Provincial Park. He already had reports of other sites in the area, and was happy to hear from me of another two. Would I, he asked, be interested in recording the Quetico sites?

It was Kenneth Kidd's vision of a systematic recording programme that launched and sustained the pro-

ject. Within the year he had enlisted the support of the Quetico Foundation and the co-operation of Ontario's Department of Lands and Forests. In the summer of '57 I recorded eleven sites in the Quetico area, and in succeeding summers added to the number in ever-widening areas of Ontario's northland. By 1961 the work Ken initiated had resulted in my recording well over a hundred sites, and extension of the project far beyond Ontario's boundaries.

So far the highest incidence of sites has been between Lake Superior and

3

the Manitoba boundary. Here (p. 3) the land is so laced with natural waterways that one may paddle in almost any direction, interrupted only by brief carries. Here is one of the continent's most accessible fishing and hunting paradises, where increasing numbers of wilderness-hungry visitors annually renew their sanity. Here privacy may still be found, and the sense of isolation; where the only mechanized sound is the reassuring throb of a Beaver aircraft on fire protection patrol. Here, in the early morning calm one may paddle around a rocky point to glide silently within hand reach of a looming cliff, and stare in wonder at the mysterious red markings of a vanished culture.

Scores of such experiences have yet to rob me of the feeling of suspense, of having been touched by fingers out of the past. Nor can all the details in the pages that follow adequately convey the intimacy of a visit to one such actual place.

The Typical Site

The photographs on the opposite page and below were taken at a small pictograph site on Twin Lakes, just north of Highway 17 and thirty miles east of Kenora. In the Canadian Shield woodlands of Northern Ontario, there are thousands of such outcroppings of rock—usually granite or gneiss—with vertical faces at the water's edge.

Few places have such large areas of bare rock as are seen here. Normally lichen growth of various sorts covers the whole surface: coarse

Photograph by Klaus Prüfer

Photograph by Klaus Prufer

leafy "rock tripe" on the upper faces; crustose types, medium to fine in texture and often of brilliant colour, on the lower and more vertical faces; and, wherever seepage is constant, a fine-grained black variety that looks much more like a stain than a lichen.

In both photographs the light areas of rock are the lichen-free ones. Here the only covering agents are the light, pink stain of oxidized iron, the occasional white streak of precipitated lime, and—rarely, as here—the mysterious red markings of the aborigine.

5

Where the lime deposits form a background the stronger paintings stand out vividly, and can be photographed in black and white successfully. Sometimes lime solutions have seeped down over the paintings, obscuring them unless one moistens them with water. Usually the iron oxide of the pigment overlies the same compound that stains the surface from the weathering of minute particles of iron ore in the rock. If, then, the pigment is weak, it is difficult to see, and impossible to photograph without colour film. Since the underlying colour is essentially the same it is doubtful whether colour filters would help to increase the contrast.

Normally the rock gets enough moisture for lichen growth. It is only when, as in this case, an overhang ensures that rain and groundwater seeping from above will drip clear of a surface that lichens are discouraged. However, a slanting rain will wet the rock beneath an overhang, so that frequent exposure to the drying action of the sun is also needed to discourage lichen growth. The Twin Lakes site has a southern exposure. Others may face the rising or the setting sun. So far I have seen only three sites on which the sun never shines. In such cases the fuzzy green lichen which often obscures them is easily scrubbed off, unlike most of the crustose types on sun-exposed faces, which are extremely tenacious. Lichens originate in a symbiosis of algae with fungus spores—both carried through the air. Such a pair, lodged by accident on the same rock nodule, or in the same microscopic pore, lead a precarious existence at best in normally lichen-free surfaces.

At water level the action of ice and waves tends to keep the rock clean. The remarkable thing is that such erosive agents seem to have had little effect on the pictographs on sites where they have obviously been so exposed for decades or longer.

As a matter of record most of the paintings are from two to five feet above the present water levels. Here, for instance, where the photograph shows me working at a tracing, they are within easy reach of a person sitting or standing in a canoe.

It is difficult to generalize about the typical location for a site. The example illustrated here marks a minor portage into an insignificant lake. We do tend to find larger numbers of pictographs on the larger cliffs facing the more travelled waterways; but this is contradicted too often by obviously important sites on small rocks in out-of-the-way places.

Only two generalizations can be made. The one colour favoured on every site is the "Indian red" characteristic of aboriginal paintings the world over. A limited use of white is made on two sites, of yellow on one, and of black on another. All sites so far found have been close to water, and all reports of sites away from the water have been traced to natural stains of oxidized iron.

The Search

How does one go about finding Indian rock paintings?

This question was uppermost in my mind as my wife, three sons, and I drove north and west early in the

Opposite:

F. H. Nohlgren reports a site on the Saskatchewan River

Ojibwa at Northwest Bay pinpoint a site on Footprint Lake

summer of 1957 to French Lake, the Canadian access point to Quetico Provincial Park. There, in a small colony of Park officers, biologists, and one botanist, my wife set up housekeeping in a small prefabricated hut while I set up my drawing table, got out my maps, and proceeded to check the reports I had brought from the Museum against local information.

That summer established the pattern I was to follow, with later refinements, for the next three years. People hearing of my work wrote in reports; I proceeded to the nearest jumping-off point, where I checked and pin-pointed the reports I had and collected new ones. Everywhere we went we talked to anyone and everyone: campers, Lands and Forests personnel, old-time residents, storekeepers, youngsters, tourist operators, and above all, local Indians.

We never knew where information might pop up. A navy recruit hitchhiking from the Yukon to Halifax gave us a location to check in British Columbia; the Twin Lakes site we got from the twelve-year-old son of a Ranger. We had no way, either, of separating fact from fancy. Reports of a painted moose six feet high turned out to be based on a tiny painting that I could cover with my hand. Pictographs on unnamed lakes were reported as being on the shore of a nearby named one.

As experience grew, a few working rules established themselves. Where there's smoke there's fire; the more smoke, the bigger the fire. Expect even the experts to disagree; all memories are fallible. And, not least, pictographs—like fish—are where you find them!

It is the original Canadians who are the best-informed in most localities. There's a special fascination about the way an Ojibwa trapper locates a site. First he will search your map with his finger till he finds the area of his registered trap line. As you watch the finger move you can tell that he is visualizing a frozen shore along his route, recalling landmarks as he searches his memory for

Photograph by Klaus Prufer

Photograph by Peter Dewdney

the one of many rock faces where former inhabitants put their enigmatical red marks. He pauses and asks for a pencil, taking the one you offer to retrace his winter trail. He stops again, and asks for something in Ojibwa. A friend pulls out a pocket knife and opens the small blade. The Indian moves the knife point carefully, then makes a microscopic mark on the exact spot—as he remembers it.

A timber cruiser or woods inspector will be equally precise; but by and large he knows of fewer sites. Yet even they and the Indians are not infallible, and cannot always place a location exactly. All are long on memory, having trained themselves by long experience to recall specific landmarks.

Access to the sites varies tremendously. Sometimes we could drive in our Volks station wagon, with canoe on top, to within a five-minute paddle of a site. At others we might borrow a "kicker"—bush term for outboard motor boat—from the nearest Lands and Forests Ranger Station for a fifteen-mile trip by water from the end of the road. And again the site might be sixty miles from the nearest road or rail. In such cases we holed up and worked on drawings until a Lands and Forests aircraft was going that way on a fire patrol or a grub run, and had room for two men and a canoe. Then they would drop us off for a few hours or a day to pick us up on their return.

During the first summer, when I was based in Quetico Park, most of the travelling was done by canoe, with one of my sons in the bow. Two

very small and unreported sites were discovered in this way; but only eleven sites were recorded altogether. In subsequent summers I took advantage of every mechanized means available, and covered three times as many sites. Nor did this preclude the location of other unreported sites. On two occasions we even spotted a site from the air!

Such a feat was necessarily rare, and exclusively the result of the general ruddiness of the rock. At a distance this is easy to confuse with a rusty orange lichen, which more than once has led us astray. The pictographs themselves are so small, and often so faint, that they are rarely visible more than fifty feet away; and on one occasion I passed a painting, while working on others in the vicinity, at least a dozen times before I spotted it. Lighting variations account largely for this kind of experience. A faint painting on a light rock, with the full glare of a noon-day sun above, intensified by reflection from the water below, can become practically invisible.

Recording Techniques

The drawings and paintings of the Shield pictographs reproduced in this book are based on direct copies of the symbols as well as on photographs. In the beginning I had no precedent to go by and had to work out methods based on trial and error.

The obvious approach was to use a grid, and at first I measured distances to key points in a painting from string "co-ordinates" stretched across the rock face. Later I changed this to light chalk marks on the rock made

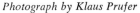

Photograph by Klaus Prufer   *Photograph by Peter Dewdney*

at the intersections of a three-inch grid. The following year, however, I found that with thin rice paper of the quality used by artists for block prints I had a material that not only became quite transparent when soaked with water from a sponge roller, but clung of itself to the rock. An outline of the painting could then be traced directly on the paper with a Conté chalk. This was a tremendous time-saver, the more so as I learned to put all the key notations that formerly had gone into my notebook directly on the tracing, using a colour code to avoid confusion of the painting with surface features such as cracks or lichen encroachment, and designations of the kind of rock, height above the waterline, and so on. In 1965, a student of Zenon Pohorecky at the University of Saskatchewan, T. E. H. Jones, devised a refinement of this technique, using Saran Wrap electri-fied with a brush to cling to the rock, and a grease or felt pencil for tracing. I have since used this method with

paintings too faint to be discerned through the slight opacity of the wet Japanese paper.

Approaching a new site I first made quick sketches of the features of each face (i.e., a rock plane over which paintings were grouped or scattered), and measured the distances between faces, designating each, from left to right, by a Roman numeral. Then I made the tracings, which could if necessary be packed away wet. Colour photographs followed, and any time that was left was spent noting such extras as compass bearing of the face, depth of the water, height of the cliff, and so on. Site numbers (e.g., Site #33) merely followed the sequence in which I recorded the sites; but do indicate an increasing accuracy due to practice.

Dating Clues

Although it was not my work to make estimates of the age of the pictographs, I was responsible for re-cording any dating clues a site might

9

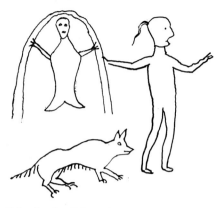

Schoolcraft, 1851; unlocated site, said to be on south shore of Lake Superior

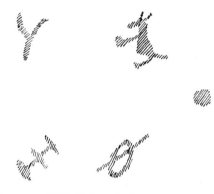

Lawson, 1885; Lake of the Woods (*see* Site #70)

McInnes, 1902; the elusive Cliff Lake Site (p. 137)

offer. Outside of skin-diving I covered all the angles I could think of, with particular attention to lichen growth, lime deposits, and weathering effects. I also noted carefully the strength of the pigment, for whatever value that might have as a dating clue.

In a number of instances sites I have recorded had already been illustrated: the Agawa site before 1850 by Schoolcraft, two by Lawson in 1885, and 18 sites by Wm. McInnes between 1894 and 1904 of which examples appear in the margin. Comparisons of these with my records should yield further historical clues. In a few cases the paintings themselves offer historical clues, picturing forms borrowed from the invading European culture.

The painting of one symbol over an earlier one is so rare in these paintings (though common in examples on other continents) that it seems of little use. More promising is the overrunning of some paintings by various species of lichen. Through studies made by Roland Beschel, a botanist currently at Queen's University, in Switzerland, Greenland, and the Canadian Arctic, considerable knowledge has accumulated of the rates of lichen growth for various species. One species, for instance, tentatively identified by Professor Beschel from colour photographs taken at .5 metres as *Rinodina oreina*, an extremely slow-growing species, has overrun the greater part of Face II on Site #27. The pigment underneath is extraordinarily strong—as strong to all appearances as the same colour freshly squeezed from an artist's tube today. If the lichen is *Rinodina oreina*

10

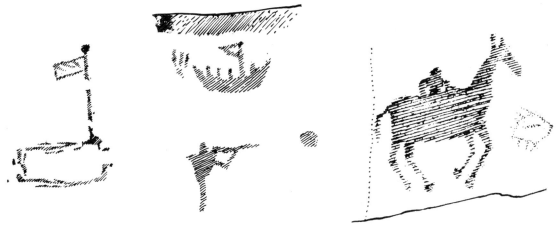

Evidence of European contact
(*see* pages 56, 42, 86)

the paint is at least a century old, yet apparently unweathered.

Lime deposits vary in thickness from a quarter of an inch to a barely discernible film. On the Cuttle Lake site a film over one pictograph is the background for another painted over it (p. 63). Since lime is a constituent (though sometimes a minute one) of most rocks, it seems likely that many of these deposits come from ground water that has dissolved the lime as it passed through the rocks. It is just possible, too, that phosphate of lime from bird droppings has been dissolved at a greater height, and re-emerged from the crack where the deposit begins. Here again are possible dating clues.

During the first summer I made a point of collecting pigment samples from smeared areas where the paint seemed thick. I was astonished to find that I could get only a few reluctant crumbs by scraping with a

steel knife. With rocks softer than granite the pigment is not so difficult to detach, but again and again I have found it so bonded to the rock that it defied my efforts to remove it. Compared with commercial pigments used in this century, the Indian paint stands up far better. In two instances initials have been painted on the same site as Indian paintings. In both cases the modern paint is already wearing thin.

A concentrated study of such factors by specialists, covering a group of sites such as the nine in Whitefish Bay on Lake of the Woods, might contribute substantially to reasonable conclusions about the age of the Shield paintings.

Interpretive and Ethnological Clues

Few who view an Indian rock painting can refrain from asking: What does it mean? Once there is any kind of break-through in dating

11

Above, and on opposite page:
Ojibwa birchbark scrolls
Courtesy, Keith Dalgettey

the Shield pictographs it will begin to be possible to relate specific sites to specific historic or prehistoric cultures. This in turn will provide some basis for working out interpretations of at least the paintings done within the last three centuries.

For there is a considerable body of knowledge about pictographic material on rock, hide, and birchbark, some of it recorded in the United States at a time when living Indians were still using, and could interpret it.

I am indebted to Frank B. Hubachek for my first glimpse of this material during a visit I made to the Wilderness Research Center in Minnesota in '57. Early in the nineteenth century, Copway, Kohl, Warren, and Schoolcraft accumulated a great deal of valuable information; this was followed by the more systematic work of Mallery and Hoffman.

Very little was then known about the Shield country north of Lake Superior, and most of the pictographs coming from the Great Lakes region were Ojibwa birchbark inscriptions from the Shield country south and west of Superior. The question arose: Were there any surviving remnants of knowledge or practice among the Ojibwa north of the Great Lakes? If so, they might be related to the Shield rock paintings and my field work ought to include a search for such material.

There were two broad types of birchbark inscriptions. Small sheets usually less than five by twelve inches were inscribed with characters that served as reminders for incantations that would heighten the owner's prowess in hunting, love, or war. These were designed for individuals who bought them from a "doctor" as "prescriptions" for their ailments. A second kind of scroll was much larger (up to six feet in length) and far more complex. This was a sort of combined textbook and prayer-book, that gave directions for the initiation ritual of the *Mi-day-wi-win* (Grand Medicine Society) and also outlined the basic *Mi-day beliefs*—all in the form of picture-writing.

At Quetico Park that first summer I had barely returned from my Basswood visit when a Park Officer, Keith Dalgetty, brought over from Fort Frances his collection of eight song scrolls, all that was left of a cache

12

of a hundred or more that had turned up years earlier on the north shore of Rainy Lake. Two summers later in the English River country I was given —for the Museum—a large Miday scroll left ownerless by the death of Francis Fisher, one of the last practising Miday "priests" in the area. And the following year I was shown one of several other large Miday scrolls in the possession of a Lake of the Woods practitioner (page 167).

Another responsibility I felt, along with a natural curiosity, was to learn what I could about current Indian knowledge—if any—about the origin or meaning of the rock paintings.

It soon became clear that no living Indian knew who made the paintings, when they were made, or what they signified. There were only the vaguest echoes of any tradition about them; most of the little I could glean was hearsay or conjecture.

It was otherwise, however, when I began to inquire about associations with the waterside rocks on which the paintings appeared. Years ago a veteran prospector, Jack Ennis, whom I had met on a bush sketching trip and stayed with a while, told me stories he had heard from the Indians of hairy-faced men who paddled their canoes into the crevices of the rocks along the north Superior shores. Jack cited these stories as evidence that the Vikings had been in the area. But it is clear to me now that he had run into the little-heeded belief in the *May-may-gway-shi*.

The word is variously translated into English. Among the Cree, where these mysterious creatures are described as little men only two or three feet high living inside the rock, the English is "fairy." Among the Ojibwa various translations run from "ghost," "spirit," and "merman," even to "monkey." When I consulted Canon Sanderson (who was born a Cree but has spent all his ministerial life among the Saulteaux and Ojibwa) for a literal translation, he said the first two syllables mean "wonderful," but he had no clue to the others. The best rendering in English I could hazard from the scores of descriptions I have listened to would be "Rockmedicine Man."

Authorities disagree on details, but some features of the Maymaygway-shi are common over wide areas. They are said to live behind waterside rock faces, especially those where cracks or shallow caves suggest an entrance. They are fond of fish, and

frequently—more out of mischief than need—steal fish from Indian nets. Since they cut the fish out of the net instead of removing them normally the Indians get annoyed. Frequently one is told of Indians, determined to put an end to this, who visit their nets in the gray of early dawn to catch the Maymaygwayshi in the act. The Maymaygwayshi, heading for the home cliff, are obliged to pass close to the Indians. As they approach they put their heads down in the bottom of the canoe. Why? Because they are ashamed of their faces. In the south and east this is because their faces are covered with fur or hair—"like a monkey" one Nipigon Indian told me, holding his two hands up so finger and thumb encircled each eye. In the north and west there is no facial hair, the shame being due to lack of a soft part to their nose.

Specially gifted Ojibwa shamans, I was told, had the power to enter the rock and exchange tobacco for an extremely potent "rock medicine." Many Indians to this day leave tobacco gifts on the ledges or in the water as they pass certain rocks—"for good luck," they usually explain.

Direct connections between the rock paintings and the Maymaygwayshi are much harder to come by. To date I have only a scattering of comments with few confirmations. A Deer Lake Indian told me, for instance, that a rock painting of a man with his arms held like this (and he held his own in a loose "surrender" position) signified a Maymaygwayshi. Another on Rainy Lake told me that the Maymaygwayshi reached their hands out of the water to leave the red handprints on the rock. And it is still a practice on Lake-of-the-Woods to leave offerings of clothing, tobacco, and "prayer-sticks" on the rocks at the foot of a pictograph-decorated face.

Another mythological creature of great interest that may also be associated frequently with the pictograph sites is *Mi-shi-pi-zhiw*, literally the Great Lynx, actually the Ojibwa demi-god of the water. At Agawa we have an authenticated likeness of this sinister deity of swift or troubled waters. In 1851 Henry Schoolcraft, the Indian Agent at the American Sault Ste Marie whose collection of Ojibwa legends was the basis for Longfellow's *Hiawatha*, published his *Intellectual Capacity and Character of the Indian Race*. Included in it were birchbark renderings of two pictograph sites painted by an Ojibwa shaman-warrior who claimed the special protection of Mishipizhiw, and proved it by leading a war party from the south to the north shore of Lake Superior. There is no room here for the material I collected in interviews about the Great Lynx, still feared and revered west and north of the Sault. But more will be said about the Agawa paintings (pages 81–85).

14

The Aboriginal Artist

Since we do not yet know when the paintings under study were made, nor of what culture or cultures they were an expression, any comments on the unknown artists must be highly speculative. It would, for instance, make an enormous difference to our attitude if we found that the paintings were the result of ten successive cultures spanning as many thousands of years, compared with the product of one culture within the space of a century. Nor do we know whether the paintings are the casual excursions on to rock of persons habitually working on other surfaces such as hide, pottery, or bark, or were done exclusively (and if so, rarely) on stone. Yet for the artist-recorder's eye the Shield sites do offer evidence of the aboriginal artist's choice of working surface, of spatial organization, of his painting media and techniques, and of his attitude as expressed in the form, content, and style of his work.

Surface and Organization

We have already noted the artist's preference for a vertical rock face close to the water. The sites themselves show a bewildering variety of locations, outside of this one factor, and so it is with the character of the faces themselves. Some are rough and pitted or coarse-grained; some are glaciated surfaces, some fracture planes from earlier rock falls. Veins of contrasting colour cross some; cracks mar others. Sometimes irregular faces are chosen within hand-reach of smooth, regular ones. There is simply no evidence of any pattern of choice.

16

When it comes to spatial organization of the material on the chosen face there is again the widest variety. Normally design concerns the artist when space becomes limited. Where *any* lichen-free vertical face suffices there is no spatial discipline: the painter can put one symbol here and another three feet away. He can begin a pictograph on one plane, and finish it around the corner on the next. At Agawa, where we know that certain symbols are related to each other, we find some separated by as much as fifty feet.

Yet the viewer will find as he turns the pages that organization and design are not entirely absent. At Cache Bay, Painted Narrows, Red Rock, Hegman Lake, and a dozen other sites there are groups of obviously related material that form compact, well-designed compositions. We even find a few instances where the natural flaws of the surface are incorporated into the whole concept, as in the example below from Crooked Lake.

By and large, however, we cannot find in these paintings any special

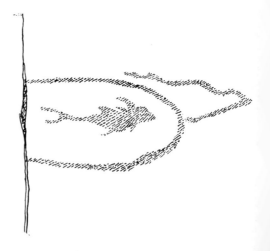

concern for either the nature of the painting surface or the arrangement of the symbols.

Painting Media and Techniques

There can be no doubt that almost all the Shield pictographs were painted with red ochres; a majority by using a finger for a brush. But what binder was used?

Red was the sacred colour for the aborigine in many areas of North America. Iron-stained earths and rusted iron ores usually occurred locally or could be obtained by trade. Colours range from a rusty orange, misnamed vermilion by some, to a purplish brick-red, varying in strength according to the proportion of clay.

On nearly every site finger-wide outlines may be found; on only a few are there lines too fine for a finger-mark; and even some of the larger forms show clear evidence that the original outline was finger-painted. Large areas were likely smeared by the same hands that left their prints on other faces.

We can scarcely suppose that the same binding agent was used by every Indian who painted a rock. But it may be that some binders were more permanent than others. Certainly most of the pigment now is difficult to scrape off with a knife. Why?

I found a clue to the answer in a non-Indian painting on the Red Rock site. Applied while dripping with the binder—presumably the linseed oil commonly used until this mid-century —the burnt sienna pigment, though still strong, rubbed off easily, leaving only a faint pink stain on the rock.

Here, surely, the pigment was so suspended in oil that it was separated by a thin film from direct contact with the rock grains.

It seems reasonable to deduce that the water-soluble fish glues or egg fluid available to the Indians would create more opportunity of contact, molecule for molecule, with the rock grains than the equally available sturgeon oil or bear grease. By the same reasoning little or no binder (i.e., water alone)—if no rain blew on the face while the paint was drying —would provide the ideal condition for such bonding.

The initials painted by the vandal in black commercial paint across the likeness of Mishipizhiw at Agawa can tell us a great deal. Dated 1937, we can already see the "red" man's paint gleaming through the weathered texture of the "white" man's. Here, facing west on the east shore of Lake Superior, the cliff is exposed to the fierce gales of the world's largest freshwater lake. Waves and shore-ice from below, a driving rain, sleet, and snow from above expose this site to extremes of weathering beyond any other. We know that the Indian paintings are at least a century and a half old. Why have they endured, still clearly discernible, for so long?

There are mysteries here that theories such as mine do not altogether satisfy. Yet common sense suggests that various techniques and materials would have been improvised as circumstances and motives varied. Some happy combinations may have endured for a thousand years where more recent paintings weathered away completely.

17

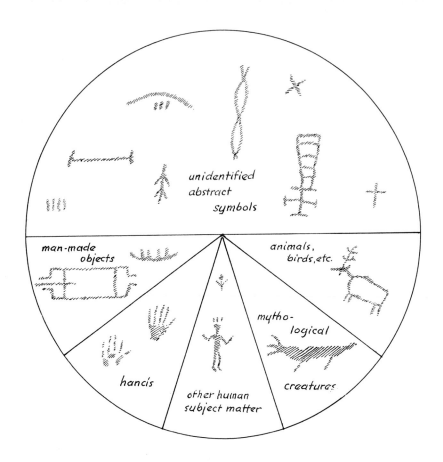

Form, Content, and Style

The diagram above forms a rough classification of all the symbols recorded in the hundred odd sites examined so far: more than 1,000 separate marks. Of these, roughly half bear no recognizable likeness to any known form and I designate them as abstractions. Many of them are single strokes occurring in groups or series that suggest tally marks. The remainder range from simple to relatively complex forms.

The other half of the symbols subdivide roughly into five groups: miscellaneous man-made objects, hand-prints, other human subject matter, animals, and composite—presumably mythological—creatures.

Do all these variations in form represent varying cultures over a wide time span, or are they the expression of a single, but highly variable, culture? Since our present knowledge is so limited we must examine them, and reach conclusions about the men who painted them, in the broadest of terms only.

We are further handicapped by the current confusion about the standards by which a work of art may be judged. It has been highly instructive to note the reactions to the Shield

18

paintings of my fellow artists (including the avant-garde types), which range all the way from undisguised boredom to real enthusiasm.

No such confusion existed in the mind of Franz Boas, whose *Primitive Art* remains one of the most intelligent and well-informed attempts yet made to evaluate the art of aboriginal cultures. In referring to the "pictographic representations of the Plains Indians" he states that "their pictography never rises to the dignity of an art." There can be little doubt that he would be even less disposed to accept the Shield paintings as "art."

Few artists would dispute that the Bushman painting from South Africa reproduced below has a greater appeal as a human expression than the Shield painting shown beside it. Yet the presence of so obvious a delight in human energy in the one contrasts so strongly with its absence in the other that we are compelled to ask why. We cannot assume that the American Indian was more stupid or insensitive than the African. We must, I think, assume that his *motive* for making the painting differed.

Here Boas has something constructive to say. In comparing the decoration of ordinary clothing among the Amur tribes of Siberia with that of their shamans' costumes he remarks, "... the painted dresses of the shamans are roughly executed. They represent mythological concepts and have a value solely on account of their meaning. The interest does not center in the form."

This gives us a useful vantage point from which to view the variations of the Shield pictographs. When we turn to the renderings of human and animal subject matter we get clear indications of a parallel trend. Out of thirty-five drawings of cervids barely half show sufficient interest in the subject to reveal whether they are deer, moose, elk, or caribou; and only five reveal the delight in form that is so apparent in the European cave paintings at Lascaux and Altamira.

We have already noted the lack of action in human renderings. When we look for facial details, or indications of hair or head-dress we find the same lack of interest, with only rare exceptions. Hands and feet are ignored or indicated in the most rudimentary way.

A second quite different tendency appears among the recognizably ani-

African Bushman painting, after Christensen

Canadian Shield painting, Quetico Lake

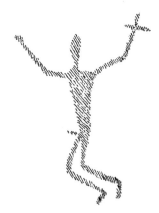

mate forms, both animal and human: distortion so startling as to be unaccountable for by indifferent draughtsmanship. This tendency leads us away from simple naturalism into a series of increasingly fantastic forms in which the forms we know are lost in a world of antlered dragons, horned, fish-tailed humans, and other nameless creatures. Beyond these forms, veiled from our understanding by a curtain of abstraction, lies the wide range of unrecognizable symbols; some of them, perhaps, simplified linear versions of dream-figures; others suggesting unknown artifacts; others again reminiscent of our own arithmetical symbols. But in even the most formal symbols, where symmetry is obviously intended, no care is taken to achieve more than a careless correspondence between duplicated forms. Nor can we say where distortion ends and formalization begins.

Considering Boas's distinction between *form*, as the visual aspect of a painting, and *content*, as the intended meaning, we may conclude that there is strong evidence in the Shield paintings of an interest in content that almost constantly overrides the interest in form. We may further suggest that the trend to distortion and fantasy relates to the Indian's known obsession with the importance of dreams.

To all appearances the aboriginal artist was groping toward the expression of the magical aspect of his life, rather than taking pleasure in the world of form around him. Essentially, however, the origin and purpose of these deceptively simple paintings remain a mystery.

20

Anthropomorphic figures,
Ontario Shield woodlands

Further Thoughts, 1967

In scanning the preceding pages for errors or omissions it seemed to me less confusing to let them stand, and merely add what subsequent experience and hindsight might suggest. For example, my earlier statement that a concern for spatial arrangement is absent from most of the paintings in Ontario must be modified by the comment that, as one moves westward into Manitoba, the examples of organized design elements multiply.

Further comments on media and technique are also called for. It is now clear, from Cree as well as Ojibwa sources, that the Shield aborigines knew how to use heat to convert the hydrous yellow ochre into the anhydrous red oxide. At La Ronge in northern Saskatchewan B-Amos Ratt described for me how he took earth from a deposit on the Churchill River, reddened it by bringing it to a white heat in a frying pan, then mixed it with oil rendered from whitefish gut. The reddish-brown paint that resulted had been used to waterproof his log cabin and paddles, and dried with a slight gloss. Later, with his middle-aged son, A-Joe, I visited one source of the pigment, apparently a rotted-out vein of iron pyrites. But there were so many impurities present that all my fire and frying pan would produce was a dark, dubious brown—no match for the old man's colour.

As early as the 1740's James Isham, in his "Observations," reported that "the Glue the Natives saves out of the Sturgeon is very strong and good, they use itt in mixing with their

Anthropomorphic figures,
Western Shield woodlands

paint, which fixes the Colours so they never Rub out &c." Both glue and oil could be got from such a source, and I suspect that the one was never wholly separated from the other so that the result had some of the properties of an emulsion. Lacking this binder the painter might have used his own spittle. This, in the shelter of the typical site, might suffice as a temporary bond, until the slower bonding action of the iron itself could take effect. On perhaps a dozen sites now I have found instances where the paint has smeared downwards as if a blowing rain had partially dissolved it before it had set. This certainly suggests a light, water-solvent binder. Geologists tell me, too, that the red oxide is partly soluble in the carbonic acid formed by rain that has picked up carbon dioxide from the air; but that it also has an adhesive action in the formation of some types of rock.

With regard to form, content, and style a few points can now be added, although a final analysis of the regional distribution of variations in these features must await completion of the whole recording project across the Shield region. Here we can point to some variations within Ontario that modify the picture provided by the pie chart on page 18. Hand forms, shown as 10 per cent of the subject matter on the chart, reach double that percentage towards the Manitoba boundary and disappear altogether in the southeast. Abstractions form only a third of the total in northwestern Ontario, but two-thirds in southeastern Ontario. Naturalism, negligible in the east, increases perceptibly in the west. Thunderbirds and snakes increase in proportion as one moves from southeast to northwest, roughly correlating, in the case of snakes, with the decreasing incidence in the same direction of poisonous species. Renderings of bison appear as one nears the prairies. Although the bush people were known to have made bison-hunting forays into the prairies, I doubt whether hunting magic was a motive for the paintings. A more promising lead was provided by two birchbark Miday scrolls that I recorded recently just west of Lake of the Woods. Their owner interpreted drawings of bison on these as guardians—along with the powerful Mishipizhiw—of the higher orders of the Midaywiwin, because it was "mighty on the prairies."

Indeed, most of the evidence suggests that the rock paintings represented dreams, and were intended to enhance their efficacy. "That's what they dreamed of, the ones that drawed," Johnny Loon told me as we sat on the rocks near his drying fishnets, just across from the Post at Grassy Narrows on the Winnipeg River. Francis Tom at Sioux Narrows was equally positive. "A lot of those guys they done some fasting where they have those paintings . . . whatever you see on the paintings that's what they seen in their dreams. I hear this from my grandfather and dad and others, too. That's why I put tobacco there." I should add, however, that for every informant that tells me the dreamer made the paintings, another turns up who is sure the Maymaygwayshi were the artists.

The Sites

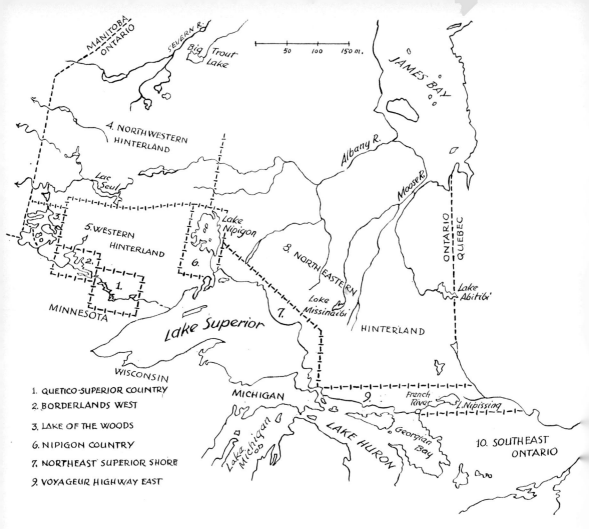

Map labels:

MANITOBA / ONTARIO
SEVERN R.
Big / Trout Lake
50 100 150 m.
JAMES BAY
4. NORTHWESTERN HINTERLAND
Albany R.
Lac Seul
Moose R.
3.
Lake Nipigon
5. WESTERN HINTERLAND
6.
8. NORTHEASTERN
ONTARIO / QUEBEC
2.
1.
Lake Abitibi
MINNESOTA
7.
Lake Missinaibi
HINTERLAND
Lake Superior
WISCONSIN
MICHIGAN
9.
French River
L. Nipissing
Lake Michigan
Georgian Bay
LAKE HURON
10. SOUTH EAST ONTARIO

1. QUETICO-SUPERIOR COUNTRY
2. BORDERLANDS WEST
3. LAKE OF THE WOODS
6. NIPIGON COUNTRY
7. NORTHEAST SUPERIOR SHORE
9. VOYAGEUR HIGHWAY EAST

Regional Divisions

The Canadian Shield rock paintings described in this book are limited to those so far recorded in Ontario and adjacent Minnesota. In the pages that follow, each site will be dealt with in as much detail as space allows. Actually, a small book could be written about any one of the larger sites.

Regional divisions on the map above are purely arbitrary, as a convenience for the reader who wishes to keep track of the general location of the site under discussion. Commencing with the Quetico-Superior region where the work began, we shall move westward along the border country to Lake of the Woods, and northward into Patricia District. From there our survey will turn eastward through the hinterland to the Nipigon country, thence to the Quebec boundary, and southeast to the huge site at Bon Echo on Lake Mazinaw.

24

I have already mentioned setting up our base camp at French Lake in Quetico Provincial Park that first summer of 1957. A few days after arrival, an airlift via the Park "grub run" brought my son Kee and me to Basswood Lake at the south end of the Park. An hour later we were paddling north, heading for Agnes Lake via Summer, Sultry, and Silence lakes, along a route ringed by pencil marks on our map that indicated the likelihood of pictograph sites (p. 3).

My diary notes on July 9 that "We have now passed through two areas marked on our maps for possible sites. There has been no sign of anything remotely resembling a pict." By noon of the following day we were out on Agnes Lake, heading south, our "hopes high, heightened by enormous cliffs on right—awesome overhang—magnificent colours." But alas: "We examined every cliff face minutely as we passed, from waterline as high as we could see, and no trace of picts. . . . no picts on the cliffs south-west of the Narrows. . . . One island was left. . . . Paddling around the east side we found a few

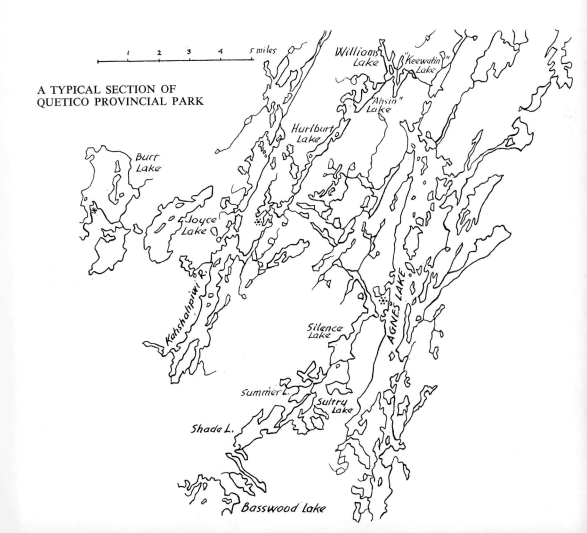

A TYPICAL SECTION OF
QUETICO PROVINCIAL PARK

Williams Lake

"Keewatin" Lake

"Ahsin" Lake

Hurlburt Lake

Burt Lake

Joyce Lake

Kahshahpiwi

Agnes Lake

Silence Lake

Summer L.

Sultry Lake

Shade L.

Basswood Lake

1 2 3 4 5 miles

undistinguished-looking faces . . . and at the base of one the barest indication of a pictograph. Kee took three colour shots and I one b. & w. I measured and sketched it." So the first—and most unspectacular—site was recorded.

We paddled north again on Agnes, I with the sinking feeling that that year's exceptionally high water had covered all the sites but this. It was with dragging paddle-strokes that we explored a group of islands in the centre of the lake. Then we were suddenly staring at Site #2: fourteen symbols of varying strength in various shades of dull red. A bear, a canoe, and several hand smears were easy to identify. The rest were too abstract or amorphous, with one exception. The latter set our imaginations going in a way that makes me smile now, but also makes me less impatient with wild interpretations from the un-initiated. To my then untutored eyes it looked like a monk and a monster together in a boat. Since then I have seen variations on the same theme: in all likelihood two Maymaygway-shi in a canoe, with upraised arms. In this case I had yet to learn the subtle distinction of shade and colour between the Indian pigment and natural rust stains on the rock, and imagination did the rest.

With two sites figuratively under our belts we set out hopefully for Williams Lake. This was the most definite report on our list. We had even seen photographs of the paintings. All reports but one agreed that they were on a sizable cliff at the west end. The exception placed it on a neighbouring unnamed lake. As the reader will have guessed we found that the minority report was right. Here we recorded three thunderbirds, a canoe, two simple abstractions, and a weird little moose. The next day we found our fourth site on the little unnamed lake between Agnes and Kawnipi.

The Neguagon Reserve on Lac la Croix, just west and south of Quetico Park, is only a few miles north of the pictographs on the big "Painted Rock." There I interviewed Charlie Ottertail, one of the few older Indians who still cherished his ancestors' ways and beliefs. The sun had set and the light was dim inside the Ottertail cabin. "A small dark room," to quote from my diary, "the frail but still vital Indian on the floor under a grey blanket, rising on one elbow to speak, sinking back between speeches . . . a lean intelligent face."

Yet there was little he knew about the pictographs: only that he was sure they had been there when the treaty of 1873 was signed.

For sheer naturalism there are no other paintings of moose that I have seen in the Shield country to compare

26

lichen

Site #4

with the three on this site. All are surely by the same hand, as is the little antelope—or deer. Unique, too, are the pipe-smoking figures; one beside an hour-glass figure and tracks, the other not far from the initials "L. R. 1781."

Each poses its mysteries.

Initials and date are pecked faintly into the hard granite. The *L* is coloured, seemingly with the identical pigment used for the pipe-smoker. The latter has the suggestion of a feather head-dress. Is it hair that is indicated on the other pipe-smoker? In Schoolcraft's glossary of pictograph symbols an hour-glass figure is interpreted as a "headless man." Yet Kohl, another early student of the Ojibwa, quotes an informant as saying: "If it were an easy matter . . . to guess what the signs mean they would soon steal our birchbark books. Hence all our ideas, thoughts and persons are represented in various mysterious disguises."

Many readers will already have some familiarity with the European cave paintings, notably those at Altamira and Lascaux. Merely a nodding acquaintance with these palaeolithic masterpieces makes it clear to an artist that their cultural milieu contrasted strongly with that of the Shield artists. Even the Lac la Croix moose lack the free-floating lines and flowing rhythms of the better cave paintings.

NOTE: pipe bowl in water colour reproduction is inaccurate; line drawing is more reliable. S.D.

Opposite:

Lac la Croix moose
Face II

And while we can no more guess at the "caveman's" conscious purpose than we can at our own aborigine's, there can be no doubt about the pleasure the former took in many of the forms he chose to depict.

Paintings of hands are interpreted by Schoolcraft as "have done"; by Copway as a sign of death. Either way we might interpret the group of handprints at Lac la Croix that surround a small, but unmistakable fox as the record of a successful war party, led by a chief with either the personal or clan name of Fox. I still

Opposite:

Blindfold Lake site,
Face II

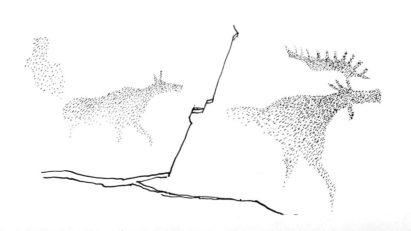

like—but recognize as sheer conjecture—my translation of the extensive smearing of pigment below this group as saying in effect: "See what we have done with the blood of our enemies!"

It was from these smearings that I scraped samples of pigment for analysis in Toronto. The findings identified the pigment as ferric oxide, but the traces of organic material which would indicate the binder were so slight that carbon-dating was out of the question. On top of that there was no guarantee that the minute quantities found did not represent stray material out of the air that had lodged accidentally on the surface of the paint. I am hoping eventually to find a slab of rock that has fallen from a site so that a microscopic study can be made of the pigment in relation to the rock grain, and to what extent and how permanently it bonds itself to the rock.

I have dubbed the pictographs illustrated above as the "Warrior Group" on the assumption that the half-length human figure is holding a weapon. Faint but fascinating material

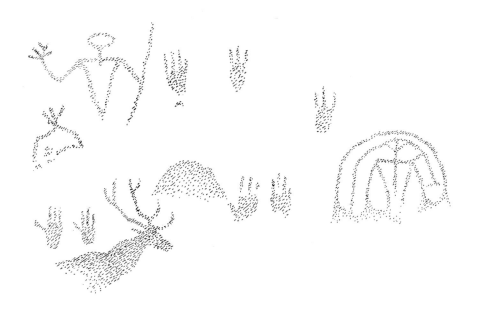

is scattered over this face: a mound-like form, a caribou (or elk?) head, and the suggestion—too faint to be certain—of a human figure in a lodge.

I recorded this site in my first summer, and was still using the tedious techniques of string co-ordinates and chalking out grids, previously described. The northern faces here could be recorded from rocks underneath; but it was otherwise with the Warrior Group and the Fox Group, painted on a sheer face that rises overhead some thirty feet, and descends an estimated eight to ten feet underwater. Here they could only have been painted from the water, perhaps in early spring from the ice; more likely in summer from a canoe.

The day we recorded them a brisk south wind brought waves sweeping vigorously along the rock face. We had a rope along the base of the cliff that gave us some control of the canoe, but my son Peter had also to make sure the canoe was not slapped against the rock. We had our hands full: he with paddle and rope, I with chalk and tape and sketch-book, while the water tossed us up and down and splashed my paper and colours with aggravating persistence.

The Lac la Croix site is in a magnificent setting: great blocks of the granite bedrock rising in steps above the water a hundred feet or more.

It is a mystery to me why not one mention in the literature has been found so far of a site on the main water route to the West, passed annually in the height of the fur-trade days by a thousand canoes.

The Crooked Lake site, on the Minnesota side of the border waters south of Quetico, *does* appear in the records, but on account of Sioux arrows stuck in a cleft high above

31

the water, mentioned by the explorer Mackenzie among others. Here, where Crooked Lake narrows imperceptibly into the lower Basswood River, a great bulk of granite leans ominously over the water, its walls streaked with a rich mosaic of iron stains, vari-coloured lichens, and vivid deposits of precipitated lime.

Here man's art is apt to be unnoticed, modestly appearing some fifty yards south of this colour display. Under one great overhang are the "Sturgeon in Net" illustrated on page 16, and nearby two horned figures. One of the latter is shown in halftone on the opposite page. The other was so faint that I failed to notice it even while working on its neighbours.

Farther along is the "Eccentric Moose," with bell exaggerated into a sort of beard; nearby a bull moose beside a pelican (?). Another pelican appears beside an unusually deep canoe with a "medicine-flag" (?) at the bow (or stern). There is an elk here; and an elegant heron beside a disc. Most interesting of all, to me, is the tree beside the lodge, within the latter a "bird-man," which Kenneth Kidd suggests could be a shaman in a steam-bath ritual. This is the only recorded Shield pictograph that clearly portrays a plant form.

Cache Bay, an extension of Lake Saganagons at the southeast corner of Quetico, was the first site Peter and

32

I recorded in '58. Here is a pleasingly compact group of human figures, canoes, and tally marks tucked away in the heart of the curl of quiet water called Lily Pad Bay, on an inconspicuous rock far from the busy highway of the voyageurs to the south.

Farther east, on Northern Lights Lake, we recorded two other sites, one of them pin-pointed for us by Jock Richardson of Saganagons Trading Post. Allan Ruxton of Lands and Forests ferried us in. Site #14 is on a high rock visible across the bay. Note the way the moose's stack is rendered in the upper drawing. Site #13 faces a channel in Nelson Bay —a scattering of somewhat obscure symbols, obviously by another hand.

There are petroglyphs, too, at Cache Bay, reported by Gerry Payne and still waiting to be recorded.

Neither Kee nor I was impressed by the rocks we passed as we paddled

Above:

examples from Northern Lights Lake, Sites #13, #14

Right:

Cache Bay group

south along the east shore of Darky
Lake's southernmost arm. Coming to
yet another rock, almost hidden by a
grove of young birch trees, we looked
up and gasped. High above the
birches a great black overhang was
poised. As we glided closer the screen
of foliage moved aside and revealed,
clear and startling, the "Heartless
Moose" with a hole where her heart
should have been, her bull calf following, the whole surrounded by tally
marks, tracks, and a vertical row of
discs.

Much else of interest was there:
the half-figure of a man aiming what
was surely a rifle, a group of canoes
protected by a likely version of Mishipizhiw, and another canoe beside
a second serpentine form, painted
across two cracks with typical dis-
regard for the painting surface.

Since then the scouts at Moose
Lake in Minnesota have reported

Darky Lake cow moose
and calf. Note splayed
hooves and dew-claws
of cow's forefoot

35

A likely Mishipizhiw at Darky Lake

another small site on the opposite shore that we had missed.

On the same trip that Kee and I recorded the Darky Lake site we paddled east to Agnes Lake, recording three minor sites that are not illustrated here. At the Narrows into Burt Lake we found extensive iron stains temptingly suggestive of an early Ford car! Nearby, however, were two genuine handprints and some other faded material. From there on we had no reports to search for, and were delighted to run across

two little moose on the waterway south of Hurlburt Lake. Finally, on the west shore of Agnes, just opposite the little island where we awaited our airlift, we found two painted rabbits, and nearby four animals that I judged to be Indian in origin: these pecked or pounded into the rock but so shallowly that we paddled past them without seeing them at first, although we knew they were there.

These are the only petroglyphs I have found to date on a vertical rock face. At Nett Lake, Cache Bay, Shoal

36

Darky Lake:
man with gun,
and projectile?

Lake, Sunset Channel on Lake of the Woods, and Footprint Lake there are other rock carvings, but all are cut into horizontal rock faces.

During my first summer in Quetico Park I heard vague rumours of a site on the northwest corner. In '58 Ernest Oberholtzer, naturalist and revered champion of conservation in the United States, told me in Ranier of a site on Quetico Lake. Later Lloyd Rawn of Lands and Forests at Fort Frances pin-pointed it for me. But it was not until '59 that Peter and I were able to hitch an airlift in to the Narrows to find the pictographs that are illustrated below. A beautifully clear group, under a low but bulky overhang, it contained a number of unusual features from the caribou (or elk) head, and one of the few human figures with its sex clearly indicated, to the long canoe in which one of the occupants appears to be standing with upright arms.

Experienced pictograph-hunters by now, we looked thoroughly along the rock faces to the east and west, and were rewarded with a second site, with two large and quite incomprehensible shapes. We finished the tracings to the distant throb of our Beaver, and I had barely focussed the camera for the first photograph when Art Colfer dropped out of the sky. I recall that trip as the one when Peter paid for our ride by spotting a thin wisp of smoke from a lightning fire far below. We circled twice before Art or I could spot it; and minutes later a radio-alerted crew was on its way from Park Headquarters to take care of it.

At least five minor sites remain to be recorded in Quetico Park, all small, but each with its contribution to make to our total knowledge.

Ely, Minnesota, is the small mining and tourist community through which is funnelled the amazing flood of

37

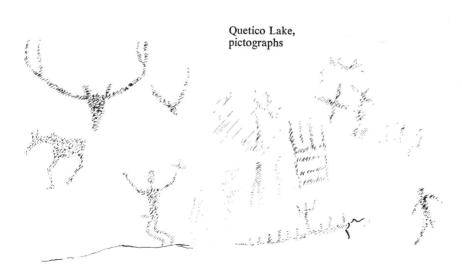

Quetico Lake,
pictographs

Hegman Lake group

Basswood Lake is the modest group of buildings that houses the Quetico-Superior Wilderness Research Center, where its Director, Clifford Ahlgren, is quietly building an international reputation for forestry research. Next door is Frank B. Hubachek, another passionate champion of conservation, a founder of the Research Center, and sponsor of many far-sighted wilderness research projects on both sides of the border. Sig Olson was among the first to bring the Shield pictographs to the Royal Ontario Museum's attention; Bill Trygg tracked down an obscure site on Island River in the heart of Superior National Forest; and "Hub" has warmly supported the pictograph recording project since its inception.

The Hegman Lake site is perhaps the most photogenic of all I have recorded. A small, well-designed group, it is painted in strong colour against a lighter-than-usual granite background. Here was the first site I had encountered that was well above the water: a somewhat awkward one to record, for Peter and André Vallières, his French-Canadian friend who was with us that summer, had to hold me by the shirt-tails so that I could lean out far enough from the rock face to focus the camera. Note the splayed hooves and dew claws of the moose which we have seen only once before, on the Darky Lake site.

As we left, André pointed out a huge, detached slab of granite below the pictures that gave forth a dull hollow sound when tapped with a rock.

On the west shore of Burntside Lake, only a short drive west of Ely,

city-surfeited Americans who each summer head north into the roadless lake country of Superior National Forest, over the border into Quetico Park, and even beyond. University professors, garage mechanics, boy scouts, and harassed housewives in their thousands arrive in Ely; some with their own gear, some to get every article and item they need from the big canoe outfitters. Most of them leave mechanization behind and go in the hard way—by canoe.

Ely is the home of Sig Olson, bushman, scholar, conservationist, whose *Singing Wilderness* quietly and sensitively renders the essence of wilderness living. Here, too, lives Bill Trygg, ex-ranger, student of Indian lore, and champion of Indian rights. A few miles north on the shore of

38

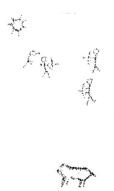

Burntside Lake warriors

young Jim Anderson showed me a most unusual site, on a small face screened from the lake by a healthy growth of trees.

"This," I remarked in my notes, "is the curiousest to date. . . . The colour is clearly different from all others and also its manner of application. One gets the impression of a dye rather than a pigment, applied with a small stiff brush . . . [some] lines have a sharp, clear edge, even where the rock is rough."

The colour was a dull wine-gray, The style, too, was different: a little group of fighting figures with bows and arrows; another group that seemed to be dancing; a head with eyes, nose, mouth, and a Plains type of head-dress. Most astonishing of all was a tiny abstraction of a moose, a masterpiece of condensation. Here, surely, close to the southern edge of the Shield, we see the influence of an impinging culture.

A short air-hop east of Ely through the courtesy of the U.S. Forest Service Center brought me to Site #17 on a widening of Kawashiwi River. Of much that was fragmentary and obscure the symbol reproduced here stood out clear though faint. An Ojibwa on nearby Tower Reserve called it a "rocking-chair"—and laughed! A Red Lake (Ontario) Ojibwa was sure that it represented a deadfall trap.

It was a long winding lumber road that took my wife and me, guided by Bill Trygg, to the Island River in the heart of Superior National Forest. Here on an imposing block of gabbro we found a small cross, and a barely discernible handprint.

Earlier, with a piece of weathered haematite, Bill had demonstrated his ingenious theory of how the pictographs were painted. Chalking a line on a granite boulder with the ore, he wet his finger and broadened the stroke to a strong, clear finger-width.

39

Kawashiwi
River, south
of Alice Lake

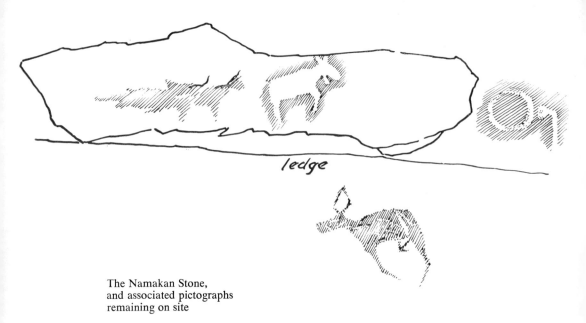

ledge

The Namakan Stone,
and associated pictographs
remaining on site

Border Lands West

Between the Quetico-Superior area and Lake of the Woods the border country pictographs thin out. In Minnesota no more rock paintings have shown up west of Hegman Lake. But there are rock carvings on Spirit Island in Nett Lake, a shallow body of water with hundreds of acres of wild rice in the heart of a thriving Indian community. Scattered over the flat rock along the north shore are dozens of figures pecked into the glacially polished rock.

On the Canadian side of Namakan Narrows, and on a nearby island of Namakan Lake, I recorded three sites in 1958. My wife and I with our seven-year-old Christopher paddled in from the east end of Rainy Lake. Our objective: a site mentioned by a United States geologist, Joseph Norwood. Conspicuous on the Canadian shore of the Narrows is a serpent-like vein of white feldspar, against a background of dark schist. Norwood, to borrow a quotation from Grace Lee Nute's *The Voyageur's Highway*, said of this that it "must be highly esteemed by them, from the quantity of vermilion bestowed on it, and the number of animals depicted on the face of the rock." This report, made in 1849, is the earliest printed comment I have yet found on a specific Shield site.

Earlier that summer we had driven from Ely to Crane Lake on the American side, in an attempt to track down persistent rumours of a site on that lake. The reports were well founded, but in an unexpected way.

40

At north
entrance,
Namakan
Narrows

At Arthur Pohlman's place I stared in undisguised amazement at a slab of rock from the Namakan site leaning against the wall of his garage: painted on it a *white* moose and a red fish-like form. Pohlman and his brother-in-law, Dr. J. A. Bolz, author of *Portage into the Past*, had found the 100-pound slab in imminent danger of falling into the water, had rescued it, and were only too happy to accept my offer to deliver it to the Royal Ontario Museum. There the Namakan Stone now rests.

The opposite page shows the way in which the stone, *in situ*, relates to the neighbouring pictographs. White pigment was also used on the peculiar symbols to the right. It looks as if the artist ran out of pigment or was interrupted while painting the large-eared moose (?) below. Whatever the interruption, it revealed his procedure in painting a large area.

Paintings on a rough granite wall around the corner are very simple—a canoe, stick figures, crosses—all badly weathered.

At the north end of the Narrows, Site #23 is painted under a wide overhang on a rock so dark that a black and white photograph would show nothing. A curious group, that seems to have a story to tell. I could not decide whether the moose's head had scaled off or had never been painted.

Site #25 is on an eight-foot wall of rock on a small island near Berger's fish camp. Visiting Mrs. Berger we found a grand old pioneer woman baking cookies for her grandchildren. She showed us hundreds of artifacts picked up on neighbouring sands during low water in the spring. The whole east end of Namakan Lake must once have been an Indian paradise.

Where Namakan waters pour into Rainy Lake we found some pigment

Site on Namakan Lake island

stains on a facing rock, but nothing we could call a site. Nor in a circuit of Rainy Lake on another occasion were we able to find any paintings on the south or east shores of Rainy.

Here in the Rainy Lake area, and along the Rainy River, evidence can be found of thousands of years of human occupation. Almost every amateur collection of artifacts in the country includes at least two or three projectile points from the Old Copper culture. At Pither's Point Walter Kenyon, digging for the Royal Ontario Museum in an ancient mound, found a copper fish-hook 5,000 years old.

Only a few miles east of Fort Frances is the Painted Narrows site, on a small island near the railway causeway. Among a number of large and very faint paintings appears the group illustrated here: an upside-down canoe, a human figure, three detached heads(?), and two weird composite figures, both with three feet. The more central of these is a perfect example of the type of strange linear figures suggestive of human or animal forms, but with dream-like appendages and projections that give them an altogether incomprehensible character. As far as I know these are unique to the Shield pictographs.

Such groupings as this and those we have already seen at Darky Lake and Cache Bay seem to have a story-telling purpose—perhaps here the record of a drowning.

Lake of the Woods

When the Lake of the Woods has been combed as thoroughly as the Quetico-Superior country the picto-

42

graph scores for the two regions should stand about even. To date I have recorded thirteen rock painting sites, two petroglyph sites and one lichenoglyph, the term I have coined for pictographs scraped in lichen-coated rock.

Whitefish Bay is properly a lake in its own right, once regarded as such by the Indians. Here half the sites are concentrated. My second purely arbitrary division takes in the lake north and west of Aulneau Peninsula; and the lake south of Aulneau forms the third.

According to some historians, the Siouan-speaking Assiniboines were migrating out of this area into the prairies from A.D. 1700 on, under pressure from the Algonkian-speaking Ojibwa, who have occupied the lake since the mid-eighteenth century.

It is a curious fact that the two sites I found the most difficult to locate on the whole lake were among the few in all of Canada to be listed

43

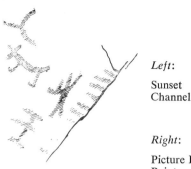

by Mallery, probably by way of Lawson, who has left us partial records of them.

By the third summer our expedition had become almost completely mechanized, depending more and more on motorboat and aircraft. In this case, though the Lands and Forests transported us to a camp-site on Sunset Channel, the locations were so vague that we took to the canoe, my wife and two sons adding three pairs of eyes to scan the shores. The first day we circumnavigated innumerable islands north of Sunset Channel, and would have been utterly discouraged but for a visit to an isolated fish camp where the fisherman told us of markings on a reef just south of the Channel. After supper that evening Irene suggested that we paddle along the shore of Cliff Island, to which we had already given some attention, just to double-check. A few miles from camp we found the group of paintings shown here.

The petroglyph site was easy to find from there; Mallery had placed it half a mile east of the paintings, and as soon as we saw the fisherman's reef at the end of the half mile we knew we had found it. This book does not cover the rock carving sites but I might remark in passing that the characters were quite different from those at Nett Lake. On Machin's point in Shoal Lake the next year I recorded further petroglyphs and pinpointed a third site northwest of Rainy Lake for a future visit.

The paintings on Picture Rock Point, Western Peninsula, are painted on a thick, rough encrustation of lime, and, with the exception of the human figure, are obscure. But here, as on most other Lake of the Woods sites, we found offerings on a water-lapped ledge: neatly folded clothing and a towel, topped by a little pile of tobacco. There were offerings, too, in a crack below the equally modest site at Portage Bay, a few miles west.

South of Aulneau Peninsula I have so far recorded only two rock painting sites. Of these the pictographs on Painted Rock Island are well known, situated as they are on the boat channel between that island and Split Rock. Sheer luck brought us to the Obabikon Channel site.

In the summer of '60 fires were so prevalent that it was an imposition to ask for help from the harassed staff of Lands and Forests. So I turned to Bill Fadden of Sioux Narrows, an experienced guide and old-timer, who took to pictograph-hunting with all the enthusiasm of a young archaeologist. Stopping over at Sioux Narrows on my way west I enlisted his help in tracking down three sites in Whitefish Bay; on my return two weeks later he had discovered three others.

Speeding up the channel from Sabaskong Bay into Obabikon Bay we caught a glimpse of red through the trees rather high up on the east shore. On shore, expecting to find another example of iron stains, we were happily astonished to discover the paintings shown here: two serpentine figures, one with antlers, the other with horns, symmetrically facing a large turtle. To the left, rather crudely painted on very rough granite, was a serpent fifteen feet long, with open mouth, ears, and three large flippers—a veritable Ogopogo.

A deep cleft between the ledge we stood on and the rock wall was almost filled with dirt and rubble. Lying on the ground were an ancient, weathered overcoat, and various rags that had rotted beyond recognition.

Northward, in Obabikon Narrows, is a lichenoglyph on a boulder, a devil-face that raises interesting questions about the original of the non-Indian painted face at the Devil's Gap, near Kenora.

The Painted Rock Island site is on a rock that projects from the slope of the surrounding shore like a great flat-roofed dormer window. Here was

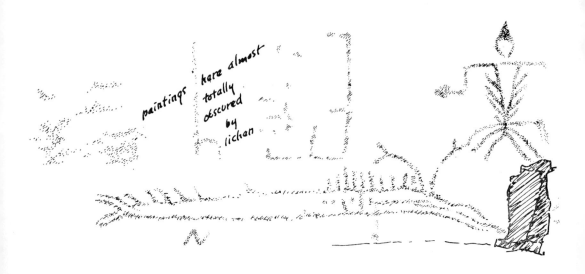

paintings here almost totally obscured by lichen

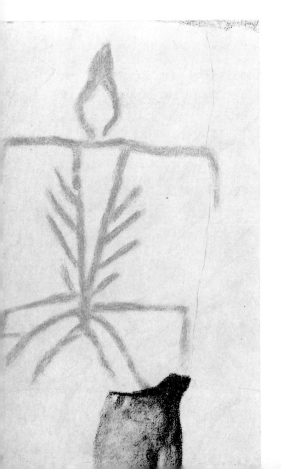

one of the few sites that faced directly north, and, as one would expect, was extensively overgrown with lichen. Fortunately most of this was fairly easy to scrub off with vigorous sponging. We found no trace of any offerings here.

This is the one site that might be related in form and apparent content to the Miday birchbark scrolls. The sacred bear stands above a rectangular structure beside a horned figure, who might represent a powerful Miday leader. A line leads directly to the typical drawing of a Miday lodge. To the right may be seen an elaborate layout of rectangular forms with "paths" from some to others.

Far to the left, badly obscured by lichen and weathering, are other suggestions of lodges or enclosures. In the centre a weird abstraction suggests a more than human form. Finally, to the lower left, floats a horned serpent-sturgeon, with projecting spines the length of its back. A most unusual painting!

46

Painted Rock Island,
detail of figure

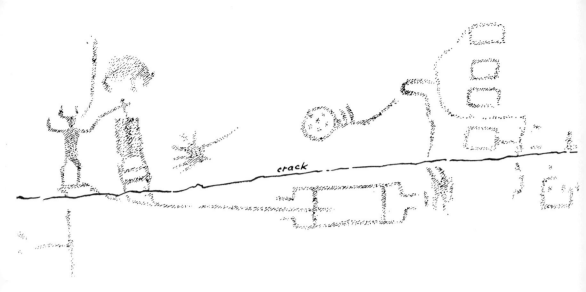

crack

It was an awkward site to record. We ran ropes down from trees high up on the shore at either end of the rock, and so secured the ends of a long, heavy pole that I could use as a rough scaffold from which to work. If I had been the original artist I should have preferred to paint this from my canoe at a time when the water was six or eight feet higher.

One item an intensive dating study might include is the variation in water levels of the larger lakes. Here, on international waters, there should be records going back a century or more, that might suggest at least a minimal possible date. Since even now there is evidence of continuing practice of the old ways among the Lake of the Woods Indians some paintings might be relatively recent. Yet the evidence of pigment erosion and lichen growth here suggest that this site is one of the older, rather than the more recent ones.

I have deliberately left the most fascinating of the Lake of the Woods

Painted Rock Island,
detail of figure

sites to the last: the cluster of seven sites in Whitefish Bay. Here the master designer of water labyrinths, after trying his hand at Quetico and elsewhere, got down to work on his magnum opus. Even old-timers stick to the channels they know; and some of the younger Indian guides have been known to get confused.

The Blindfold site, some miles north of the Bay but on the same side of the lake, I had known as a boy. Bruce and Dorothy Johnston, summer campers from Winnipeg, had sent me, via the Museum, the location and a description of the Sioux Narrows site. But rumours and reports from various sources of at least two of the other sites gave only the vaguest locations, and I am quite sure that without Bill Fadden's knowledge of the bay and keen interest in hunting for sites I should still be looking for at least a couple of them.

Strangely, few residents, summer or permanent, knew of these paintings. Actually, unless one is paddling, or drifting in an outboard motorboat, the passerby has a poor chance of seeing anything interesting along the shore. It is a sad commentary on our holiday habits that speed has become such a mania that we are denying ourselves some of the greatest pleasures to be found in such waters, not least the thrill of rediscovering for oneself these mystifying remnants of prehistory.

Yet I keep reminding myself that as a boy at the Blindfold site, inter-ested though I was in the Indian past even then, it was the offerings I saw on the ledge below that stayed in my memory. Perhaps the very incomprehensibility of these paintings tends to close off our interest. Certainly the Blindfold paintings are as difficult to read as any others.

What, for instance, is the affair on a tripod to the lower left? A drum? If so, it is quite unlike the Indian drums we know of today. In the centre (not illustrated here) is a crude little moose, whose forebody has almost disappeared under seepage that may offer a dating clue. On the extreme right of this face a monstrous form beneath two upturned canoes suggests the sinister Mishipizhiw.

The real interest, however, centres in the symmetrical grouping shown on the opposite page. A moose, undoubtedly, on the left. But what kind of a creature do we see on the right?

I could not resist the temptation of placing underneath this creature one recorded in the Lake Baikal region of south-central Siberia by A. P. Okladnikov, a U.S.S.R. archaeologist who has made extensive studies of rock paintings and carvings in Eurasia. The finger-painting technique, the curious protuberance on the snout, and the crested back all provide an amazing coincidence of conception and execution. It would be ridiculous, of course, to assume even the most tenuous of cultural links.

About three miles southeast of Sioux Narrows Post Office, facing

48

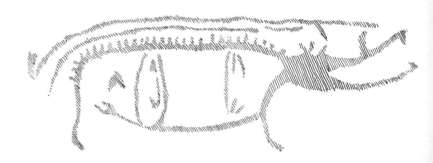

A drum?

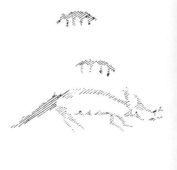

An early European fort?

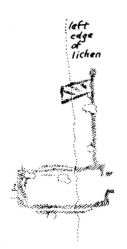

left
edge
of
lichen

west at the northern end of a bulky outcrop of granite is Site #28. Big blocks of rock-fall at the base of the site gave me a footing for the recording work, as they probably did originally for the painting.

The drawing in the top left margin is surely an Indian's impression of an early European fort, such as La Vérendrye may have built on Massacre Island. How else can one interpret the flag, with a ball on top of the mast, and the suggestion of a pattern on the flag itself? The triangular pennant flying from the mast of an unusually deep and heavy-looking "canoe" strongly reinforces this impression of an intruding culture.

On Face II we see handprints, a small man beside a serpent-monster, the latter with jaws and fore-flipper, and what appears to be a deer in a canoe. That the latter is not so strange a concept to the Indian as it might be to others is demonstrated in birchbark pictographs illustrated and interpreted in Densmore's *Chippewa Customs*. Here two families are shown, each in its own canoe. In the one a large bear is followed by three small ones, with a catfish in the stern. In the other three eagles are followed by a bear. The animals represent the clan of each person, the children inheriting their father's clan. It is interesting to note that the old Indian fashion, now disappeared, was for the head of the family to take the bow position, as a hunter logically would.

I recorded this site in the summer of '58. Two years later, on the way to greener fields with Bill Fadden, I stopped off as we passed it to take further photographs. In the interval

50

since my last visit someone had placed some clothing, a bundle of sticks, and tobacco on the rocks at the base. The sticks were thumb-thick, peeled, and daubed with red and blue paint. What could they mean?

While I was out west, Bill made enquiries of the local Ojibwa and was told that these bundles were placed on the rocks with clothing and tobacco when someone was sick, different colours being placed on the sticks for different illnesses.

We found similar "prayer-sticks" on three other Whitefish Bay sites and nowhere else. Are these a survival of an ancient practice, or the result of a recent cult among the quite numerous non-Christian Indians of the area? So far as I know no other instances of this practice have been observed. In Shoal Lake, where Presbyterian Christianity is dominant, only one Indian had heard of the practice, and seemed not too well informed about its significance. Much remains to be learned here.

If I had had any doubts about the connection between the pictographs and the offerings, they were resolved at the three other sites. In the Devil's Bay site, the Annie Island site, and the one just south of Devil's Bay, the offerings were always directly below the pictographs, as here.

Bill Fadden had also been told that there were always just forty prayer-sticks. In the two sites where the bundle was intact this was true; in the others the binding string had rotted and some of the sticks had floated away in the water. Bill also remembered seeing an old Indian in a bark canoe with his family many

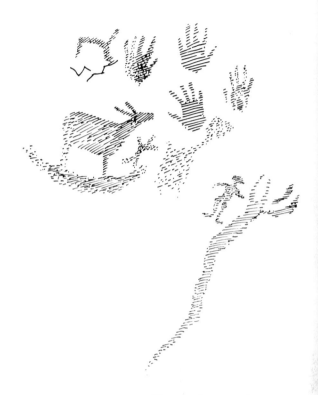

Above, and on opposite page:
Face II of Sioux Narrows site

years ago flinging water with his paddle on the rock at the Devil's Hole and talking loudly, as if to an unseen person.

The site on the northeast point of Hayter Peninsula had a different kind of surprise to offer—two, in fact. The

51

first was a new kind of symbol, which from its obvious resemblance to a checker-board I was inclined to eye suspiciously. Yet it was in the authentic colour, and the squares were filled in an irregular fashion. Had the two appeared in a European cave they might have been dubbed "tectiforms." They do suggest, for what it may be worth, a weaving texture. Here there were no prayer-sticks; but an old china cup and other odds and ends were visible in a horizontal crack nearby.

Our recording work done, I was just packing cameras and kit when I noticed that Bill was still scanning the rocks. It was a novel experience to work with someone more anxious than I to find another pictograph. Bill pointed to a rock that stood above and back from the waterside face we had been working at. A most unpromising place; I gave it only a careless glance.

"Would that be anything up there?" Bill wanted to know, pointing to a rusty stain halfway up the other face. A couple of hand and toeholds took me up easily enough—and there was another group of paintings!

Whoever had painted them must have had some difficulty, or have been very short-sighted; for to lean far enough out to focus on the rock, standing on a mere bit of a ledge, one needed both hands. Fortunately Peter was along that day, and we had lots of rope. Bill anchored the rope at the top of the cliff, and Peter, with a bowline around his shoulders, had both hands free to work on the tracings and photographs as I handed up the materials from below.

At the north end of Annie Island we almost missed the sole but fascinating pictograph on a beautiful granite wall: a vertical zig-zag of

Undeciphered paintings
25 feet above the water,
Hayter Peninsula site

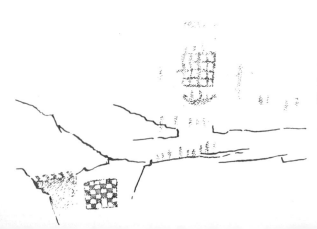

52

finger-width colour that ended in the head of a Maymaygwayshi. Among the rocks below, like a shorebird's nest, we found another deposit of clothing, prayer-sticks, and tobacco, all as fresh as if they had been put there yesterday. Small wonder that we nearly missed the painting, for the wall was streaked with black lichen whose edges were scalloped in rhythm with the undulations of the pictograph. (See page 154.)

The same day that we recorded these two sites we hunted high and low for a site in Devil's Bay. It was a beautiful day and we found the obvious rock, but though we scanned and scanned there was nothing on it. Two weeks later we returned and found it immediately in the centre of the self-same rock, very faint but clear. So much for the effect of glare on visibility!

Apart from being somewhat larger than any thunderbird hitherto recorded, there was nothing too notable about this site.

I have yet to learn why Devil's Bay is so named. Yet in Sabaskong Bay there is a small rocky island in the centre of which is a huge "nest" of boulders, obviously an artifact—though a laborious one—and the island is named Devil Birdsnest Island. Indians as far east as Lake Nipigon refer to such constructions as "Thunderbird's Nests." I have heard of others, but this is the only one I've seen.

The Devil's Hole is no more than a deep, almost horizontal fissure, averaging about five inches in width, in the granite outcrop just north of Devil's Bay on the west shore of the

Devil's Bay
thunderbird

53

Annie Island
site, associated
with "prayer sticks"

southern arm of Whitefish. The adjacent paintings seem to be merely smears, except for one small abstraction. Some seventy feet farther south is a far more interesting group: a series of large abstractions that have an unusual consistency of style and dimensions, but leave the viewer clueless. In the fissure, I ought to add, which goes farther back than the eye can see, are traces of offerings, fragments of chinaware, and so on.

By far the most interesting feature of Site #105, just south of Devil's Bay, is the bison. In the summer of '58 I got wind of a site on Mameigwess Lake said to have a buffalo represented on it. Though it was off my itinerary I drove in from Highway 17 west of Ignace to have a look at it, arriving at Jorgensen's

camp in a heavy rain. The Jorgensens not only treated us to lunch but lent us their boat and heavy slickers to run across the lake to the site.

In driving rain, with little shelter from the overhangs, Klaus Prufer and I photographed the main features. It was disappointing to find on my return to do a proper recording job the next summer that what we had taken for bison on our first visit was actually a moose.

The first unmistakable bison I found painted on a rock was far to the north, on the Bloodvein River. Here on Whitefish Bay, and a bare hundred miles east of bison country was another. This is not as accurate a drawing as the Bloodvein Bison, but more alive. Another seems to have been painted to its left, but it

Devil's Hole, Face Ia

flake

flake

flaking

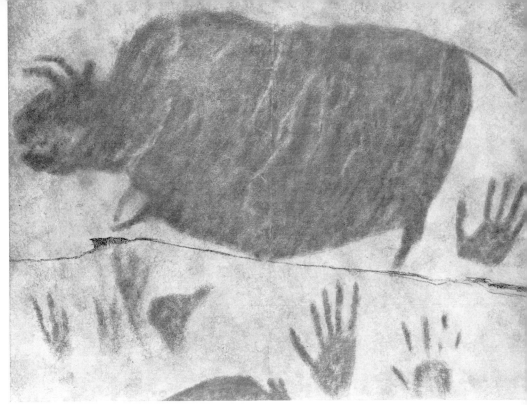

Whitefish Bay bison
(*see also* page 98)

is impossible to tell whether rock erosion or deliberate distortion accounts for the peculiar neck and head.

Two animal forms and a baker's dozen of handprints make up the other markings. On a ledge below was a most handsome offering with prayer-sticks. We carefully lifted one corner of the neatly piled clothing to find that it was all clean and in good repair. No attempt had been made to foist off second-rate articles on the mysterious healers.

An impressive armada sailed from Sioux Narrows on August 8, 1959: the flagship, a big Lands and Forests diesel, bearing myself, Irene, and Christopher, following the Johnstons who had pin-pointed the site earlier in the summer, and a third high-powered motor launch bearing American friends. An hour later the flotilla lay to in a maze of islands in the centre of Whitefish Bay, completely "at sea." Nevertheless we finally made our way through the labyrinth to the most remarkable site of the summer, on appropriately named Picture Rock Island, which we mistakenly identified at the time as Fergus Island.

For individuality of setting this was supreme—an eagle's eyrie rather than an artist's easel, fifty feet and more above the lake. The red of the paintings is clearly visible 500 yards away.

55

Then, as one approaches, the red disappears behind the lip of a twenty-foot-wide ledge.

Looking up that day the place seemed inaccessible; a sheer drop to the water protected that approach completely and there was no way down from the top. However, with the will there proved to be a circuitous way, and the biggest difficulty was in getting water up for the tracings.

On Face I the turtle, unusually naturalistic compared with others elsewhere, is clear and strong. The undulating form in the centre, which may have lost significant details under the lichen, repeats a theme that occurs with variations on six other sites—notably the Annie Island site we have just looked at. The ladder-like form and the handprints are said by some non-Indians in the locality to refer to a raid on Ladder Lake by the "Red Hand," a band of marauding Indians in Minnesota in the 1880's or '90's. On Face II the reversed brackets with vertical bar between is a form that will be seen again at Red Rock and Pictured Lake. Is the animal canine, with the Samoyed tail of an Eskimo dog? If so, it is very recent, for the only dog known to the early natives hereabout was a small hunting animal. Yet it may not be a dog at all; we have already seen how readily, for reasons unknown to us, natural forms could be distorted.

A child's handprint appears among the others—or is it simply a small painted hand? On this site it is difficult to tell whether the hands were printed or painted. I can offer no comment on the baffling form at the centre right.

56

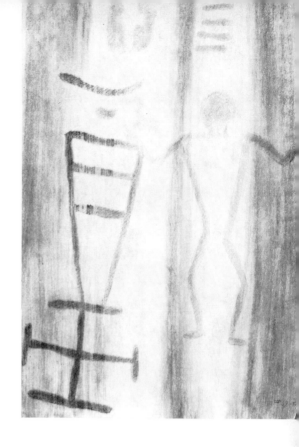

Face III has three exceptional forms. The lower left figure seems intended for a bird: note the suggestion of feather tips on the wings. The ladder–Maltese-cross character in the centre and the seeming combination of two abstracted animal forms on the right are typical Shield abstractions. But the faint, lime-obscured human figure is almost a brother to the central figure at Blindfold, and shares with half a dozen others the artist's curious disinclination to close off the lower part of the body.

It should also be mentioned that the rock itself is most unusual: a smooth concave curve of glacially sculptured granite. The pigment seems indissolubly bonded to the rock—for how long is anybody's guess.

Northwestern Hinterland

The arbitrary division we have made between western and northwestern hinterlands follows the northern line of the C.N.R. through Minaki, Sioux Lookout, and Arm-

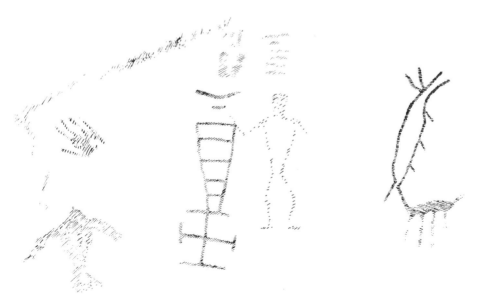

strong. Although each year roads snake their way farther north of this line into the untouched wilderness, quick access has been almost entirely restricted to air travel. Of an estimated total of sixty important sites in the region only a third have been recorded. The whole vast area is currently administered, for forest protection, wild-life study and control, and so on, from Sioux Lookout. Fires raging in this area during the summers of 1960 and '61 have made airlifts for other purposes impossible, and all we have in the pages that follow is a sampling of the total, most of them collected during the summer of 1959.

In the neighbouring Shield country of northern Manitoba I already have the same scattering of reports that prefaced the finding of many others in Ontario. A brief reconnaissance trip I made to Lac la Ronge in northern Saskatchewan tells the same story. Much remains to be done.

The northernmost reported site in Ontario is north of the fifty-fourth parallel on the Sachigo River, near Manitoba, a site I paddled past unknowingly on a trip with my father in 1928. This site and four others were reported by Edward Rogers, anthropologist at the Royal Ontario Museum, who with his linguistically gifted wife, Jean, spent the better part of a year with an Ojibwa band in the Round Lake area. Farther south I owe John Macfie of Lands and Forests the locations of a dozen sites from Artery Lake to the Vermilion River. Finally, the ubiquitous McInnes turned up sites at Cliff and Route Lakes.

One of the luckiest breaks I had in the summer of '59 was the chance to fly with Jake Siegel, the Lands and Forests pilot at Red Lake. A superb flyer with a widespread reputation for fire protection, he was the first man I've met who literally wouldn't hurt a fly; Peter and I saw him carefully herd one, trapped in the takeoff, across the windshield with his hand to the open window—and freedom! For such a man the fire that destroyed millions of living creatures was a personal enemy. The following year on the evening of my arrival at Red Lake I learned that he had made twenty-five separate flights that day, carrying in men and supplies.

I should make it clear that I could only get airlifts by prearrangement with headquarters, and only then if a Beaver aircraft were going in the same general direction that I needed to go, on an assigned fire patrol or fire tower grub run.

The great advantage of pictograph hunting by aircraft is that in a single circling of a lake one can spot every likely outcrop, and unstrap one's canoe fifty feet from the likeliest, saving hours of shore exploration.

Cochrane River Face VI

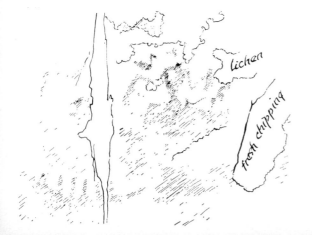

Of the nine faces on the Cochrane River site, a few miles north of Deer Lake, and the most northerly site I have so far recorded in Ontario, all but the first, fourth, and fifth show only vestigial traces and are not illustrated here. It is a pity that this site is so remote. Faces VA and VB offer almost the full range of dating clues: over-painting, lichen-encroachment, exfoliation, and a wide range of pigment intensities and hues.

The most interesting drawing is the winged figure, unfortunately obscured on the right side of the head by chipping. A bird with a human head? Was the head originally symmetrical, with the appendages on either side representing a special hairdo? Whether so or not, we shall find two human figures on the Bloodvein River site that suggest the same idea.

While at nearby Deer Lake waiting for the plane to pick us up I spent two hours interviewing John Meezis, one of the older Indians, and a third hour at the school. The summer teacher, Miss Todd, let me take charge of her seventeen children (ages six to fifteen) for a drawing experiment. The great majority, when asked to draw a moose, a fish, a bird, and a man, produced what any other Canadian schoolchild might have drawn. But four of the older children drew female figures as hour-glass forms with appended head and limbs; and three of the four drew the arms in a surrender position.

The Bloodvein River site was one of those rare experiences that are the supreme reward of pictograph-hunting. Here, some eighty miles northwest of Red Lake, in the Lake

Cochrane River
pictographs

59

Winnipeg water-shed, was a beautifully proportioned bison, and a
human figure with the most detail I
have yet recorded.

There was much else beside: the
two curious "wigglers" on Face I,
the canoe on Face II with figures in
the same manner as on Lake Nipigon
and far to the south at Site #2 on
Agnes Lake in Quetico Park. Face III
is a puzzling conglomeration of over-
painting and abstractions in which
little can be deciphered. I would guess
that the animal on the upper left is
a porcupine.

The northern exposure was unexpected, and the question arises how
the rock came to be lichen-free at
the time it was chosen for a site.
Peter and I scrubbed off whole yards
of the fuzzy green species that had
grown over a good half of the
paintings.

Note the hair-do on the little man
on Face II, very like that on the
Cochrane River "Eagle-man."

On the opposite page is a copy of
the Bloodvein bison. The site is perhaps a hundred miles north of the

parklands where the bison herds once
roamed; but the artist shows a
familiarity with the animal that suggests either frequent hunting excursions southward, or his own southern
origin.

There seemed to be—and I so
recorded it—a vague indication of
the heart in this bison, but I was still

60

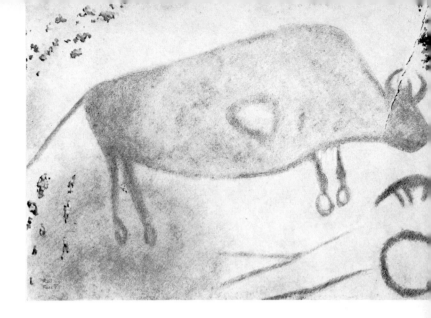

Bloodvein
bison

puzzling over it when it was time to go. The photographs convey the same impression without being any more decisive. A peculiar feature of the feet is the way in which the hooves are rendered as ovals. I was startled a few months later, leafing through a book on the Lascaux cave paintings, to find exactly the same treatment.

Overleaf the "Bloodvein Shaman" is illustrated. I so dubbed it the following winter after going through all the Ojibwa birchbark drawings I could find recorded in the literature. Frequently in the scroll pictographs zig-zag lines like those emerging from the head of this figure are interpreted as thoughts or magical power enter-

61

Bloodvein shaman

Face II (*see* text, page 61)

ing, or emanating from, the person's eyes, ears, mouth, or head. Again, on a number of Miday scrolls the Miday priest is shown holding the otter-skin or other medicine-bag from which he and his fellow Midaywiwin "shoot" power into initiates.

The lines at the side of the head I would guess to be the same kind of hair arrangement as we see on Face II and on the "Eagle-man," but in more detail.

The large canoe beneath and the porcupine to the left might represent the fighting prowess and clan of the shaman. But I must emphasize that these are only guesses.

The Sharpstone Lake site was spotted from the air by Peter while Jake and I were looking in other

62

Lower Manitou Narrows (*see* page 74)

Cuttle Lake, detail of lichen and pigment, Face I

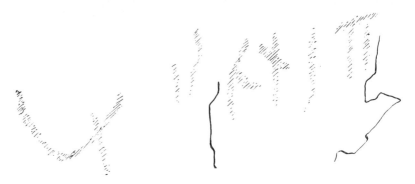

Sharpstone Lake site

directions for a hearsay site we had picked up from a Little Grand Rapids Indian. It provided a wide shelf of rock that made an ideal landing-dock for the plane while Jake waited the half hour it took to trace and photograph the rather sparse, faint markings. Since I stood in a foot of water and could barely reach the higher paintings this was obviously painted from a canoe when the water was higher. Some of the painting has gone; for here, as so often occurs with granite, large slices half an inch thick had flaked off by exfoliation. Had there been more time we might have found a slab or two with pigment on it in the shallow water; but the wind was changing, and Jake's plane was in no position to ignore the fact.

We were very thankful for the accuracy with which a Red Lake Indian pin-pointed a site on a little

sliver of a lake west of Rex, north of the English River. Luckily enough the lake was too small for the pilot to chance a take-off with Peter, myself, and canoe aboard. Consequently we made a rendezvous for the end of the afternoon on Rex Lake, and on the way there spotted a second site.

Site #65 was next to a waterside rock shelter where Peter slept in the shade while I recorded the modest group of two handprints, a circle, an upside-down canoe, and a few other vague markings. Site #66 was an even more modest one: only a handprint, tally marks, and two vague figures.

At Grassy Narrows, and southward at two sites on Delaney Lake, we recorded two likely Maymaygwayshi, a rudimentary moose, and a cocky little turtle that had a very human look about him. The real pictograph find of the summer was

Sites west of Rex Lake

Samples
from
Delaney
Lake

not on any rock, but inscribed on a seventy-inch birchbark scroll, left ownerless by the death of the last great Miday practitioner in the area, Francis Fisher. Twelve human figures, all armless, and six water creatures appear on this, quite unlike anything in the rock paintings. But two bears are rendered in an identical way to those shown on the Shield pictographs.

When Chief Tabowaykeezhik learned of the existence and purpose of the Museum he gave the scroll to me, along with the late Miday "priest's" medicine bag, to be preserved for posterity in Toronto.

White Dog, just off the English River, is the only site where the local Indians had any interpretation to offer for the pictographs. The animal (painted in the usual red ochre) was a white dog, the human figure a woman. This came out while talking to a group on the dock to which our Beaver was tied. "How can you tell it's a woman?" I asked one Indian. He drew himself up with some dignity to reply: "I am a *man*."

At another place and time a Nipigon Indian told me of the "White Dog Feast" in which a small dog was eaten by members of the Midaywiwin as part of the ritual: "They don't say, we're eating a dog. They say we're eating a bear. They don't cook it very much—they eat the blood and everything—but I heard they drink medicine before." The bear, I might add, is the central figure of the Miday ceremonies.

My second visit to Red Lake yielded a site on that lake itself, to which I was taken by Bob Sheppard, a Provincial Police Officer who had an unusual interest in, and understanding of, the local Indians. The site was small and close to the water,

Left:

Grassy Narrows

Right:

White Dog

Red Lake pictographs

Route Lake
pictographs

on a face that sloped outward at such an angle that I had quite a time getting the paper to cling to the rock.

The Red Lake highway runs past Cliff Lake, on which McInnes recorded a site I have yet to track down. With the help of Joe Vocelka, who runs a popular tourist camp there, we reached the one site known on the Lake. "Lots of paint but little to decipher," my diary notes. "Disappointed, we poked the nose of our borrowed craft into every bay and inlet except the northwest arm where, we had been assured, there wasn't a rock you could spit at. Not a sign of McInnes' site. . . " (page 135).

Before it was flooded Lac Seul was one of the paradise lakes of the north, with countless sandy beaches, great stands of white pine, winding creeks, and lush swamps where the wild rice grew thick and thousands of ducks bred. Here were endless miles of browsing for moose, and latterly deer, with depths where great sturgeon and fat lake trout lurked. With the flooding at least five pictograph sites disappeared; and the only clue to what they were like is in the peripheral ones. The Old Copper people were here, and who knows what other wanderers before them. Archaeologically the surface has barely been scratched.

Here I spent two idyllic summers in my late teens, and paddled south on one occasion to pass within yards of the Route Lake paintings. Years later, staring at the pair of figures shown on this painting, I was as mystified as any reader will be. What strange subtleties of aboriginal culture were manifested here?

66

Route Lake, detail

Until recently the area between Lac Seul and Lake Nipigon north of the C.N.R. has been as difficult of access as other parts of the northwestern hinterland. However the new road from Sioux Lookout to Armstrong will open up the Pickle Crow road, and be of great help in recording the sites reported in the area. Flying out of Sioux Lookout I have been able so far to record only four which must suffice to represent the many others.

I have John Macfie to thank for his meticulous sketches and notes on the Vermilion River site just south of Carling Lake. Here, though there is only a sprinkling of badly weathered drawings, the setting is most unusual. In an alcove of the glaciated granite, against a glistening white reredos of encrusted lime, the little red markings appear like tiny icons. Passing Indians still leave tobacco in the little niche that is shown below.

A geological survey party ran into two sites on Vincent Lake while I was in "the Sioux" and passed them on to the District Forester. There was

Left:

Vincent
Lake

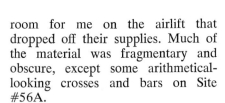

Right:

Schist
Lake

room for me on the airlift that dropped off their supplies. Much of the material was fragmentary and obscure, except some arithmetical-looking crosses and bars on Site #56A.

Reports of sites in the Savant Lake area were too vague to justify an airlift. But I had, as I thought, a fairly reliable location on Fairchild Lake, one of a confusingly similar series filling a thirty-mile east-west fault. Flying south from Carling I spotted a promising glow of red on a rock 800 feet below. We landed long enough to verify the site, then high-tailed it for home in the threat of a gathering storm. I made a sketch of the landmarks from the air, assuming that this was Fairchild Lake. How wrong the assumption was became clear two days later when we flew over Fairchild in an Otter. Buffeted by one rain squall after another we vainly scanned the lake below for landmarks that weren't there. The site turned up ten miles west of Fairchild, on Schist Lake—an unreported site that we had found by sheer mis-management!

West-Central Hinterland

From Lake of the Woods eastward to Lake Nipigon, south of the

68

Carling Lake (Vermilion River)

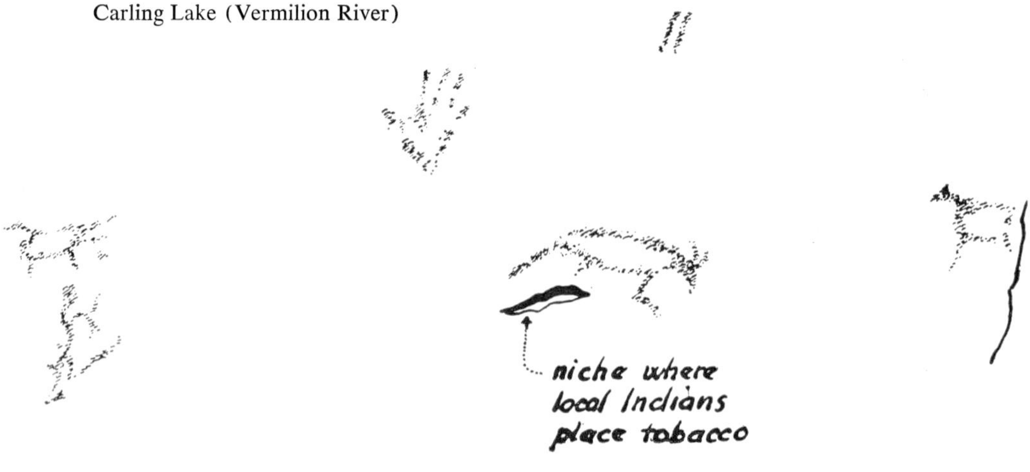

niche where
local Indians
place tobacco

northern line of the C.N.R., there is road access to within an easy water journey of most of the sites.

It was a great time-saver, however, to fly into Dryberry Lake from Kenora, and to be able to survey the outcrop locations from the air, before picking the most likely one to land beside. In this case we had only the name of the lake to go by, and a guess by a man who had heard that it was in the north end of the lake. But the sites we had picked from the air were unrewarding and it was many a weary mile that Peter and I paddled, encouraged briefly by finding one slight site on the north shore, before we moved into the northeast arm and finally sighted a huge, low overhang on the west shore.

As we approached, the whole face glowed with red colour and I knew we had located McInnes' site. What we saw was much as he had recorded it. Only the "eagle" was missing from his drawing, a puzzling feature, for if it had been painted since his visit it

would reasonably have been in the strongest colour on the face, and the contrary was true. The answer seems to be that McInnes ignored the forms that were indistinct, and perhaps also those that were puzzling to him. But we must also remember that he was there as a geologist, and that all kinds of interruptions were possible to make his record incomplete.

The serpentine form here we have seen in various versions before, but nowhere else in outline. The bird form which I have guessed to be an eagle looks rather more like a loon, erect and stretching its wings on the water. However, unlike Gertrude Stein who wrote, "A rose is a rose is a rose," the Indian would be more likely to say, "A bird is a loon is an eagle is a man is a manitou!"

A greater contrast in the mood of Mameigwess Lake could scarcely be imagined than the day already mentioned when we photographed it in a driving rain, and the day of our return. This time, as we approached

69

Dryberry Lake site

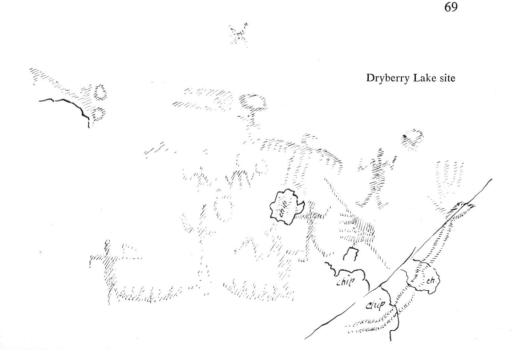

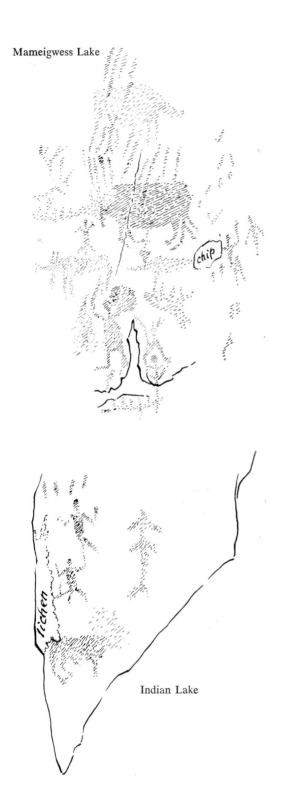

Mameigwess Lake

chip

lichen

Indian Lake

by borrowed kicker from our road's-end stop at Camping Lake, the day was hot and sultry and the water still as glass.

We entered the east end of Mameigwess Lake in an uncanny stillness that was somehow enhanced by the crystal clarity of the water, where even at two paddle-lengths depth we could see the sandy bottom, and watch small schools of pickerel swimming deep below.

When we looked closely at our "bison" there could be no doubt about its having been intended for a moose. Thin lime deposits had all but obliterated the identifying head and bell. Yet it remained an intriguing pictograph, surrounded as it seemed by flying spears. And were the hind legs drawn in two positions to convey a sense of motion?

As it stands we cannot be sure whether the second pair of legs might not have been intended for arrows. With the almost standard lack of motion in animal renderings on nearly every other site the former is most unlikely.

What the psychologists call projection is a real problem in recording these sites. For instance, on my brief visit to the Jorgensens the previous year they had mentioned a man with a bow and arrow, and I was sure I recognized one at the time. Yet on my return neither Peter nor I could find even a hint of one. The temptation is particularly strong in cases like this where obscurity and over-painting contrive to suggest all manner of combinations.

A letter I had from R. H. Neeland of St. Thomas, Ontario, has some

70

interesting comments to make on a visit he made to the lake, then called Rangatang, many years ago.

"Our guide, who knew the local Indians, said that he had tried to get some explanation of the pictures from them, but had been told that they had been on the rock face long before their time. They were unable to give any reason or explanation. They added that there was a devil at the foot of the cliff and they were not going past unless absolutely necessary."

The consensus of opinion among the many Ojibwa I have interviewed is that the Maymaygwayshi were more to be avoided than feared. But there seems to have been a special fear associated with this site, having something to do with a large recess in the rock near the main group of paintings. White residents say that a *Weyn-di-gow* is believed to inhabit this "cave." It is an interesting fact that nowhere in the Shield country have I found evidence of Indian use being made of such caves as there are. This contrasts with sites in the Alberta foothills where I have recorded pictographs in two rock shelters and had reports of others.

The paintings on nearby Indian Lake offer no startling novelties. They were likely painted from the ledge they stand above, whereas the Mameigwess site must have been painted entirely from the water. There is the suggestion of a fishtail on the two Maymaygwayshi delineated, which tallies with the belief of some southern Ojibwa that the Rockmen lived under the water.

The Turtle River sites, south of Highway 17, both at the second rapids below Bending Lake, one above, the other below, were reported to me by my fabulous Fort Frances friend, Roscoe Richardson. The paintings would be rather dull if it were not for the handsome turtle. Here a typical distortion adds a grotesque touch—apparently a canoe is emerging from the turtle's body.

The turtle, too, raises the interesting question of whether the river got its name from the painting, or the painting its subject from the river's name.

The Cuttle Lake sites are so close to Rainy Lake that they might easily have been included among the border pictographs. When Art Colfer dropped me off on his way from Fort Frances to Nym Lake, Quetico Park,

Turtle River tortoise

71

early in my second summer in the field, I already had some misgivings, for though he had taxied along the length of the only cliff on the lake I had seen nothing, and I was going in on the strength of veteran timber cruiser Bill Bergman's memory of a site he had noticed thirty or forty years ago.

I paddled back and forth twice along the shore before I noticed one little group on an obscure face. Looking for a place thereafter to make a fire and heat a can of soup for lunch, I happened to look up at the only angle from which I could have spotted them—a mass of iron stains on the rock high above the water, normally masked from view by a small stand

of trees. I scrambled up the fifteen feet to the ledge, pushed through the trees—and there was a beautiful sight!

Up to this point every site had been easily accessible from the water. Here I had problems. First, how to build a scaffold to reach the paintings from the ledge, without an axe to cut poles or rope to lash them. Second, how to supply myself with water for tracing with no container other than a small soup tin!

Here were the first clear examples of overlapping I had seen. Here, too, was the first, and greatest, encroachment of the slow-growing *Rinodina* over an extremely strong pigment. And here I learned that the pigment

72

Cuttle Lake site
(*see also* page 63)

Cuttle
Lake
detail

#27 62 (71)

could be transparent; where the deer's feet overlap the canoe beneath, only the interposition of lime seepage in the one case proves which came first (*see* colour plate, page 63).

Only a few of the symbols were new: the forms that one might describe as inverted suns, and the most curious little demi-human centaur-like abstraction.

Two days earlier I had recorded an equally rewarding site, on the narrows south of Lower Manitou Lake some twenty miles farther north. This had been recorded by McInnes some seventy years before and I have

73

Above: Minor site, Cuttle Lake

Below: Centaur-like abstract

Lower Manitou Narrows
(*see also* page 63)

McInnes' drawing, 1890

reproduced his drawing on this page for comparison with what I saw.

The central question raised is whether McInnes omitted the strange figure so conspicuously absent in his drawing, or whether he lacked time to put it in after recording what he considered more important. The square with the headless man is easily identified, and the viewer will note that there are only vague traces in my drawing of the chain of figures McInnes shows to the right.

Moving eastward, the next hinterland site is a most obscure one on Lac des Mille Lacs. Almost vanished, little can be seen except the remnants of a crude little headless human figure. But Fred Peters, a local resident with some Indian ancestry, had a story to tell about its origin. When a boy who had gone off with another lad failed to return, his father went to the conjurer whose business it was to locate missing things, or persons, through his use of the "shaking-tent."

"Well," said Fred "he [the conjurer] told what's happened. Those boys is not dead they's living, but you'll never see them again. A few days after, this man was fishing and then he seen the drawings on the rock. So then he thought the boy was in the rock there. They stole the boys—Maymaygwayshiwuk did—canoe and everything. And that," Fred concluded, "is pretty hard to believe."

Only twenty miles southwest of Fort William is one of the most individual Shield sites on record. A short winding stream from Oliver Lake takes one into tiny Pictured Lake, surely a mere century ago one of the

74

Pictured
Lake samples

most out-of-the-way spots imaginable. The theory that the pictographs were associated with important canoe routes breaks down on this example completely.

Here, except for the Burntside Lake example, is the only rock painting in the Shield where eyes and mouth (or nose) are shown, on a kind of dog face that is itself unique, and is made more so by a tiny man with outstretched hands faintly discernible between the ears. To the right on the same face is a circular figure, with feet but no head.

On Face II is the most remarkable painting of a canoe I have yet recorded, illustrated below. If we could trust proportions a dugout is suggested. More important, the heads, shoulders, and elongated torsos are clearly delineated, as well as a bow and stern paddle. On this same face is the name "simo" and the same vertical stroke between reversed brackets that we noted on a Whitefish

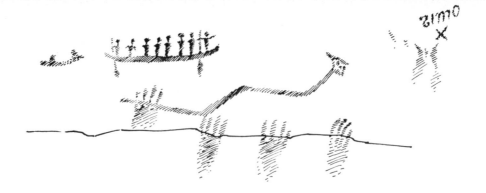

Bay site. It is a moot question whether the "simo" was painted by a semi-literate *coureur de bois* living with the local Indians, or an Indian who had learned in his contact with traders or missionaries so to render his own name. In any case the form of the letters, for all the backward *S*, is remarkably well executed.

Finally there are the serpent and the finger-smears. Again we find eyes, in the triangular head. Was our hypothetical *coureur de bois* standing by with suggestions, or did he perhaps paint all these characters?

The Nipigon Country

At the mouth of the swift, deep Nipigon, almost opposite the community of Red Rock, on the east shore of the river where it is already widening to enter Lake Superior is the major pictograph site of the area. Peter and I reached it by courtesy of a Great Lakes Timber tug that charged and hammered down the bulky British Columbia boom logs, churning through two acres of boun-

cing pulpwood to bring us and our canoe to the boom-beleaguered shore. Scrambling up a spiky deadfall we reached the ledge from which the pictographs were painted, a hard stratum of the reddish sedimentary rock that outcrops along this part of the Lake Superior Shore.

Influenced, no doubt, by the orderly arrangement of the rock layers, the symbols appear in neat succession along some fifty feet above the ledge—extraordinarily like an arithmetician's nightmare. The squatting figure that was painted from the shore below is surely a Maymaygwayshi; the more so as Lake Nipigon Indians informed me of the old belief in an underground channel that led from underneath this figure directly through to Lake Nipigon. This accounted for the Maymaygwayshi being seen up in Gull Bay with huge trout freshly caught in Lake Superior!

Notable here, too, are two examples of the reversed brackets enclosing a vertical bar. Another

76

Nipigon River Maymaygwayshi

example of this occurs far to the north on Wunnumin Lake in a contemporary lichenoglyph of which George Hamilton of Lands and Forests sent me colour photographs.

The pin-pointing of four of the Nipigon country sites I owe to Keith Denis of Port Arthur, the indefatigable historian-bushman and conservationist whose canoe has been up-ended over more portages north of Superior than anyone else's I know or have heard of. It was he who gave me my first report of the Orient Bay site, and confirmed the report, by Mallery out of McInnes, of a site on Echo Rock, on the northwestern shore of vast Lake Nipigon. I am indebted to him, too, for other sites remaining to be visited in the hinterland west of Lake Nipigon, as well as one on the Superior shore south of Agawa in Mica Bay.

Site #33, only a mile south of what was once the Prince of Wales' fishing lodge on Orient Bay, was a real puzzler. Beside a handful of what were obviously Indian abstractions in

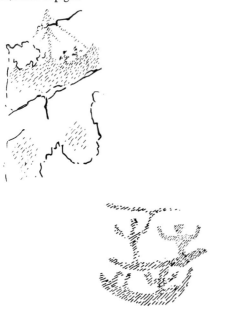

Kaiashk Bay

In the summer of '59 through the most welcome co-operation of the District Forester at Geraldton, Peter and I were passengers on the spacious, diesel-powered Lands and Forests work-boat whose beat was Lake Nipigon. Heading northwest we crossed the big lake to Gibraltar-like Echo Rock, a great mass of granite that pyramids up from the shore, then drops sheer to the lake.

The pictographs are weathered almost to the disappearing point either by ice action or by exfoliation. The centre of interest, as well as the least undecipherable, strongly suggested to me an Indian's impression of a York boat, with a mast amidship, a suggestion of stays, and two plainly visible crewmen. As the reader probably knows, Lake Nipigon Indians were in contact with the French fur traders, notably Radisson and Groseilliers, as early as the mid-seventeenth century. The evidence is startling at Gull Bay, where I talked with heavily bearded blue-eyed men whose native tongue was Ojibwa.

Just south of Gull (or Kaiashk) Bay the shore is lined with three or four miles of cliff averaging twenty feet in height. Norman Esquega ran us along this shore in his small fish-boat to record three small sites, all illustrated on these pages. Here again I was on McInnes' trail. Yet he was either in a hurry, just jotting down sketches as he went, or he had not developed the more careful renderings of separate groups characteristic of his Red Rock and Lower Manitou and Dryberry drawings.

That the Echo Rock boat was intended for a large one is evidenced

red were the faded outlines of a square-tail trout, black along the dorsal outline, white along the belly. I recorded it with reservations, confused by the naturalism of the colour and proportions. In my report I summarized it as "influenced" by European standards. A year later, through Keith Denis, I talked to the artist's niece, who well remembered the painting in its prime—a handsome rendition of the trout in full colour, that had been retouched from year to year. The artist had no Indian blood, merely summered in the Bay between 1912 and 1924. Since then I have eyed any colour but the Indian red with double suspicion!

78

here, for in these two-man canoes men with arms upraised in the same manner are far larger in proportion to the canoes than the crew of the Echo Rock boat. It is just possible that a widely travelled Nipigon Indian, seeing—let us say—the newly launched "Griffin" on Lake Huron with its hairy-faced crew, thought he was staring at a startling new manifestation of the Maymaygwayshi. The strange thoughts that passed through the mind of such a man on such an encounter we can never know; but like all men he would rationalize what he saw in terms of what he knew or believed.

A case might be made for the theory that the coming of the hairy European might have influenced the aboriginal concept of the Maymaygwayshi. Along the borderlands west of Superior these "rockmen" have hairy faces, and again among the Montagnais-Naskapi of northern Quebec. The northwestern Ojibwa speak only of fleshless noses, and the Manitoba Cree of dwarfs. What spoils the picture is Jenness's reference to the belief of Parry Island Ojibwa in a smooth-faced Maymaygwayshi—though their bodies were thought of as hairy.

All such speculations aside it is well established that most North American aborigines, unlike Europeans, regarded both facial and body hair as a blemish and went to great pains to remove it.

Kaiashk Bay examples

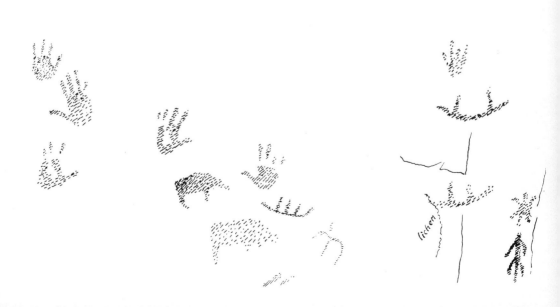

Courtesy, the Telegram, *Toronto*

The Northeast Superior Shore

The prevailing winds blowing across the world's largest fresh-water sea pile great waves by summer and ice masses by winter on the rocks that line a rugged and little-travelled shore. Yet this was the route of the fur brigades a century and a half ago; and the Puckasaw pits, recently excavated by Norman Emerson of the University of Toronto, testify that men lived on these shores thousands of years ago. With the opening of Highway 17 floods of the wilderness-hungry are coming north, lighting their fires where voyageurs and Indians long ago lit theirs.

In 1958, however, Mike Kezek's Trail's End Lodge at Montreal River was literally the end of the road. Thither on a Saturday morning in September four of us drove the ninety miles from Sault Ste Marie for a rendezvous with Mike and his thirty-five-foot launch: Gordon Longley, Assistant District Forester, Dave Carter, *Sault Star* feature writer, his wife Ann, and I. In Mike's sturdy lake cruiser we watched the Lake Superior shore go by: the long smooth curve of sand-edged Agawa Bay—calm in an off-shore wind—the cluster of rocky islands off the promontory to the north behind which Agawa Rock lay hidden, and to the west the vast sweep of Superior, broken only by the low mass of Montreal Island.

At Agawa even in the calm the water was restless beside the sloping ledge under the sheer cliff and Mike anchored his boat well away. We commandeered a leaky punt from the fish-camp on a nearby island, and paddled ashore with one oar, a piece of plank, and a bailing can. Then, as my diary relates, "I stared. A huge animal with crested back and horned head. There was no mistaking him. And there, a man on a horse—and there four suns—and there, canoes. I felt the shivers coursing my back from nape to tail—the Schoolcraft site! Inscription Rock! My fourteen months' search was over."

Soon the ledge was alive with flashing camera bulbs and busy feet. Gordon took charge of measurements, Dave took roll after roll of film, Ann carried things, while I plastered pictograph after pictograph with rice-paper and traced, traced. Offshore, Mike anxiously watched the manoeuvrings of Mishipizhiw in the form of an ugly rock that loomed out of the crystal depths uncomfortably close to his anchorage swing.

We were shocked by the crude initials splashed in black paint over the central figure; only recently I learned they were the work of a fisherman's teen-age daughter. But there were two consolations. She had dated her "work" 1937, and already the black was weathering into oblivion, the Indian's red showing through beneath.

We have yet to identify the Chingwauk who gave Schoolcraft the bark drawings and interpretations of this site. It might have been Shinguaconse, widely known warrior in the 1812 campaign, but more likely Hatcher's learned Indian, Shingvauk, "who understood pictography." If the latter, we can more easily understand the discrepancies between his memory

81

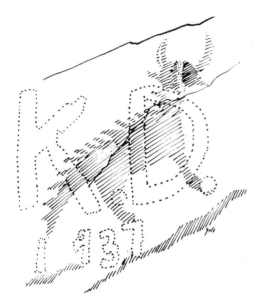

"The fabulous night panther and great serpent"

Does symbol to right of horse signify a turtle?

drawing and the original, especially where he added details missing in the Agawa original.

We offer here for comparison what seem to be the relevant pictographs on the Agawa site and a reproduction of Chingwauk's drawing.

Chingwauk spoke of a south-shore shaman-warrior named Myeengun, "who was skilled in the Meda [*mi-day*]" and thus acquired the influence and prestige that enabled him to organize a war party "which crossed Lake Superior in canoes. . . . The results of the expedition [are painted] on the face of a rock at Wazhenau-bikiniguning Augawong . . . or In-scription Rock, on the north shores of Lake Superior, Canada. . . . The passage was made in five canoes. . . . The first was led by Kishkemunasee, or the Kingfisher, (6). . . . The cross-ing occupied three days, depicted by the figure of three suns under a sky and a rainbow, (7). . . . Number 8 is the Mikenok, or land-tortoise . . . which appears to imply . . . reaching land. Number 9 is the horse. . . . The Meda is depicted on his back crowned with feathers and holding up his drum-stick . . . used in magic rites. Number 10 is the Migazee, or eagle, the prime symbol of courage. In Number 11 he records the aid he received from the fabulous night panther . . . and in Number 12 a like service is rendered to the credit of the great serpent."

82

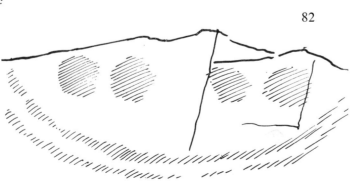

Symbols at site suggesting "four days over the water"

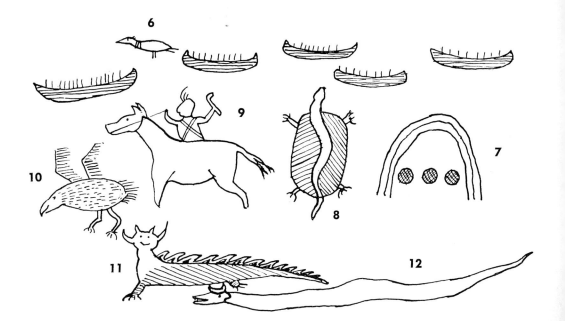

Schoolcraft's
reproduction
of Chingwauk's
recollection
on birch bark
of the Agawa
pictographs

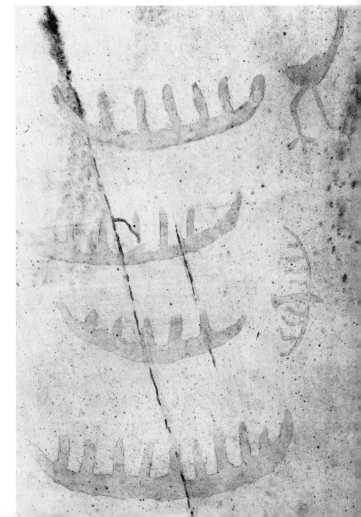

Detail of
canoe group:
upper canoe
is "led" by crane,
third canoe
by a flying bird

Copway's inventory of pictorial symbols interprets an arch as meaning "sky," and an *inverted* arch as "water." Chingwauk's memory reversed the more appropriate water sign into the one for sky, and recalled the four days as only three so that his interpretation ought to have read "four days over the water."

Since the opening of Highway 17 north of the Soo the Lake Superior Provincial Park staff has built an access road and stairway so that the public may reach and view the site for themselves by land, at least on calmer days when the rocks are dry. Potential visitors are advised to take time to look carefully; it is easy to walk past some of these paintings without noticing them: especially when one has half his attention diverted by Lake Superior rollers lapping at the ledge. "Santa Claus and his reindeer" (as they were first reported to me) are rather far along and difficult to reach. The second version of Mishipizhiw is on a ledge that can be reached only by water.

I strongly doubt whether the deer have any connection with Myeengun's paintings. There is, indeed, a naturalism here that we must travel all the way to Lac la Croix to duplicate. The reclining deer, in my opinion, is the masterpiece in this regard—a difficult subject rendered almost delicately in a clumsy medium. Whatever this group may mean, the forms show a real delight in the subject for its own sake, and the style owes nothing to other rock paintings. The peculiar boat-like sleigh with one occupant again has no parallel in other Shield paintings.

The Agawa horse reproduced in line on page 80 not only indicates that Myeengun was a poor horseman, but provides a major dating clue. It is recorded that the first horse arrived in Quebec in 1647, followed by fourteen more in 1665, dubbed by the Indians "moose of France." When did the first military horses appear in the Great Lakes region? Or had Myeengun been to the plains?

But for the pictograph-hunter the burning question is the location of the south shore site. Schoolcraft places it "on the banks of the Namabin, or Carp River, about half a day's march from its mouth." This fits the Carp River in Porcupine Mountain State Park, Michigan, where a seven-mile long escarpment of a sort of sandstone rears more than 200 feet above the rough little river. Other Carp rivers along the south shore seem less promising.

84

Second version of
Mishipizhiw

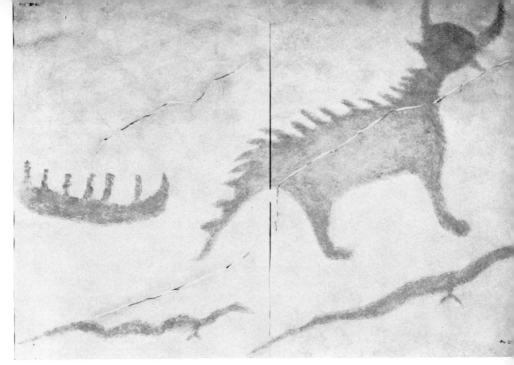

Detail of Mishipizhiw, serpents, and canoe
(disfiguring initials were not included in painting)

Reclining deer
(half-size)

The country bordering the Great Lakes is big and rough, and sites tend to thin out. Inland the lakes increase in frequency as the country scales down; but not till we get into the Gogama-Timagami areas do we find the thick spattering of lakes so characteristic of northwestern Ontario.

In the northwest corner of this hinterland, on the very edge of the Shield, I recorded a modest site at Terrier Lake. "A poor site . . . two handprints, a possible human, a few dots and lichen-spotted abstractions," my notes sum up.

Lumbering has been going on in the region for many years, and a depressing number of sites, notably those at Manitowik, Horwood, and Lady Evelyn lakes, have been drowned out by lumber dams. Fortunately one of the major sites is still accessible, the Fairy Point pictographs on Lake Missinaibi.

This was the site I had tried to sketch from the canoe on a trip with my wife. Seventeen years later I was back for a more serious effort. Vince Creighton, wild-life authority with a strong urge for archaeology, was with me, and Harry Tuvi, the local Lands and Forests ranger.

The water was even rougher than I had seen it on the previous visit. According to my diary Tuvi drove us close, "spattering spray and wallowing in the deep troughs. As we neared the cliffside it was obviously inhospitable, but we went close and I jumped on a wet, sloping rock with the rope in hand. A jerk on the rope from the boat—and it was let go, or go in. So I was marooned for five minutes till they could manoeuvre the boat close enough for me to jump back." Out on the railway years before they had warned Irene and me of frequent drownings off Fairy Point, of a big bull moose that had been "sucked down" at the place. When a brisk wind blows across the long southwest arm, building up big waves that bounce off the rock wall to make an ugly cross-chop, the tales don't sound so tall.

Faces VI and IX are illustrated here. On the latter it is not difficult to identify a caribou; the other animals are more debatable. The intriguing creature with open mouth,

Detail
of Face IX
Lake
Missinaibi

Fairy Point, Face VI

single, curved horn, and somewhat reptilian body I would guess to be a rendering of Mishipizhiw. On the other face there is little that can be understood.

Most of the symbols shown on these facing pages are mystifying, too. Is a feather head-dress indicated on the human figure, or rays of power? The little moose shows an attempt (as a sort of afterthought?) to render the two farther legs. The white crosses (not shown here) display the only white pigment outside of the Namakan site. On Face VIII there is a curious little figure that reminds me of the "centaur" on page 73. The figure with the three tally marks at the top suggests a horned man, but unfortunately is too vague for any reliable impressions.

88

I have already mentioned Jack Ennis, the prospector with the stories of Vikings on Lake Superior. I met him on my first paddle in to Lake Missinaibi, and it was he, on learning that I was an artist, who suggested that I look for the paintings on Fairy Point. On a later occasion when we had a few days together in a mining camp east of Heron Bay, the subject came up of the deep erosion fissures in the rocks along the Superior shore. It was then he told me of Indian traditions of having seen "red-haired men in big canoes who used to paddle right into the cracks in the rocks."

I suspect that the idea of red hair came from Jack's urge to prove the Viking stories. If one asks an Ojibwa a leading question like "Did they have red hair?", the answer is all too

Fairy Point, Face IV

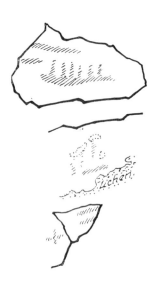

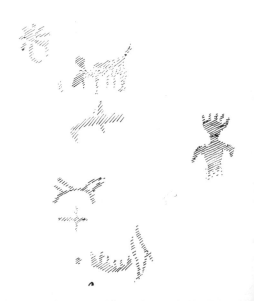

likely to be a courteous affirmative, and if the interviewer is obviously naïve an Indian will get some quiet pleasure out of agreeing with anything he comes out with. In any case I have found that the Indians I have interviewed are much less concerned than I with such details; their verbal descriptions, like the pictographs, take it for granted that the audience will do some filling-in on its own.

I have yet to find an Indian who is not puzzled by the name of Lake Missinaibi. The Ojibwa prefix *"miss"* or *"mish"* means large or great, but the last two syllables seem meaningless. It's a long shot, of course, but my own theory is that "Missinaibi" might be a corruption of *mu-zi-nu-pay-hi-gun,* a word Canon Sanderson of Red Lake gave me as the best

Ojibwa for a painted pictograph. In any case, so many things can happen from the time the surveyor asks a local Indian for the name of the lake to the time when it appears in print on a topographical map, that the wonder is that so many are intelligible.

An example of how easily one may jump to the wrong conclusion is provided by the name of the nearby railway station and Post Office, Missanabie. The assumption I made twenty years ago that this was a variant spelling of Missinaibi was corrected by an old-timer who recalled that the place was named after a Miss Anabie, a popular construction-camp nurse during the building of the railway.

One would expect, in the vicinity of such a large site as that on Fairy

89

Fairy Point, Face VIII

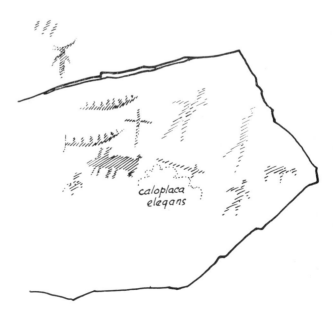

caloplaca eleqans

Point, to find other smaller ones. In nearby Little Missinaibi there are three such sites; and Manitowik Lake, where another site has been drowned out, is only a short hop to the southeast. However, flying over the country from Chapleau, I could see very few lakes where sites were even possible; and in fact over the past three years no further reports have come in.

The Little Missinaibi sites were reported by W. T. (Bill) Hueston, then District Forester at Chapleau, who took a strong interest in them. My diary refers to the scale map he sent me "on which all three sites were exactly pinpointed, so there was no

Little Missinaibi site

trouble but the wind, which made Site #76 particularly wet to work on."

Site #74 was not too exciting. It is interesting, though, to compare the clumsy human figure on it with the tiny Maymaygwayshi type on #75 underneath an enigmatic abstract combination.

The triangle of hinterland enclosed between White River, Sault Ste Marie, and Sudbury is strangely empty of pictograph sites, or even rumours of such. My wife and I searched vainly for a petroglyph site south of High Falls near the Vermillia River on a confusing series of rock ridges just south of that river. Bill Hrinovitch, who went with us, had seen it twice, while hunting in the fall.

Farther east, in the very heart of the eastern hinterland are the Ninth Lake and Scotia Lake sites, which are illustrated on the opposite page.

Ninth Lake, on the East Spanish River is a short air-hop east of Biscotasing, for several years the home of Archie Belaney, the fantastic character who as a small boy in England wanted to be an Indian when he grew up—and did, as "Grey Owl." One can still hear colourful stories about him at Bisco where he made his picturesque transition from white trapper to "Indian."

The current water level at Ninth Lake was so low that the tip of my steel tape, when I stood in the canoe stretching it up at arm's length barely reached the upper limit of the pictographs; and toeholds were too slim for climbing. So I could only measure and sketch the paintings, and had to take my photographs from an oblique angle. This is the site where, through

90

Comparison of symbols

no one's fault in particular, I was stranded alone for thirty-six hours, with my canoe for a shelter, a tarp for a bedroll, a small tin of soup for meals, and—by luck—a small bottle of instant coffee!

This site, and one on the Upper French River that we have yet to discuss, were both beautifully pinpointed for me by Al Supple, woods inspector for K.V.P., a well-known pulp and paper firm.

The Scotia Lake site was reported as early as the fall of '57, but it was three years before Peter and I, with Chuck Thompson at the controls, flew in to Camp Friday, on Lake Onaping, where we met our correspondent, Stig Stromsholm. In-

terviewing an Indian woman who was working for him, I asked her if she knew anything about the Maymaygwayshi. "That's an animal that comes out of the rock where the pictures are," she told me.

The Ninth Lake site offers us a neat little group of symbols: the sort of formalized drawings—including the thunderbird motif—that lead one to suspect that they might have been derived from quill work on moccasins or baskets. It is interesting to compare the upper right symbol with a rather similar one on Painted Narrows, and I have invented, to sharpen the similarity, a possible transition form. Yet one must be suspicious of such theoretical ingenuities.

91

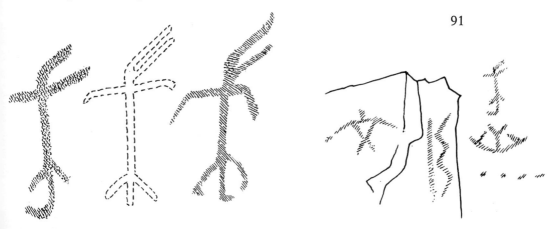

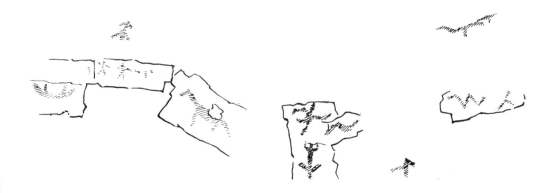

The Scotia Lake site is saved from a certain monotony of rudimentary forms—perhaps human—by the rayed head. In Schoolcraft's inventory we find a "warrior bold as the sun" that is not dissimilar (p. 91).

It was early in the summer of '59 that Irene, Peter, Christopher, and I pitched our tent on the desolate shore of Upper Grassy Lake, deep in the Gogama forest. Here a disastrous fire had left only a few gaunt, weather-bleached pine sticks standing above a tangle of deadfall and second growth. A strong wind whipped up the fine sand that once had been covered with forest humus, till there was sand on our bedrolls and even between our teeth. Across the lake lay an Indian's cabin, with the morning's wash flapping in the wind against a background of scrub.

Peter and I put the canoe into the water and found one little site; mostly tally marks and finger-draggings, but there was one little Maymaygway-shi. We had hoped, driving in, to borrow a Lands and Forests boat and kicker at Ronda, but the only available one had just broken down. So we decided to paddle in to Ferris Lake, variously described as seven, nine, and eleven miles away. It turned out to be fifteen, following the maddeningly tortuous curves of a sluggish stream, or crossing swampy lakes where shifting grass islands made the map useless.

"At last," announces my diary, "Ferris Lake, and down its length to find the site. A most peculiar one: little blocks of slaty schist with figures and symbols—a horse(?) and a dinosaur (!) and a human figure or two. Fortunately I could work from a ledge and recording went fast."

It was a weary crew that waved to the aging Ojibwa couple outside the lone cabin on Upper Grassy as we paddled past their place in the gathering darkness. Early the next morning, when I went down to the lake to wash, there was Thomas Nephew, our neighbour, wearing the

friendliest of smiles. I had one more site to record on this lake, and asked him to go along.

"It was a joy to have an Indian in the bow—an unusually good canoeman, even for an Indian. And I was lucky to have him along, for most of the site was exposed to the waves and we had a wild time taking tracings and measurements. When I ran out of film it was too wet and rough to try reloading. So, back to camp— Nephew's sixty-nine-year-old strokes as powerful as a young man's, in a quick rhythm that tired me. . . . Talking to Nephew I learned that he portages seven miles and paddles twenty to Gogama for Church services. He has lost all knowledge of Ojibwa beliefs, apparently . . . knew nothing of the Maymaygwayshi."

Until I succeed in pin-pointing a rumoured site on Lake Abitibi the Gogama cluster will remain the closest to the Quebec boundary. Inside Quebec, near Lake Kippawa, I have a reliable report of petroglyphs. Farther east, in the upper watershed of the St. Maurice River, Jacques Béland has reported a number of rock paintings. Doubtless, the Shield woodlands of that province contain many more.

A definite report, via Macfie and others, of a site at Diamond Lake took us in to Lake Timagami a few days before we did the Gogama sites. Peter and I flew in to Bear Island where we interviewed eighty-year-old George Turner, son of the former Hudson's Bay Company factor, one of the most knowledgeable men in the area, though only part Indian.

Confirming the Diamond Lake site, he also pin-pointed three sites on Lake Timagami itself. Our Beaver dropped us off at Diamond Lake just long enough to do a job on it. The rock here was a fine-textured off-white quartzite, an ideal background for the pictographs. Lake Diamond had been flooded, too, judging by the one group that was largely underwater.

A clumsy heron, the vestiges of a possible Maymaygwayshi, and a number of stick figures appear on this site. The circle with centre marked we have already seen at Cuttle Lake. Both Schoolcraft and Copway include it in their inventories: the former as "a symbol of time," the latter as "spirit!"

Site #80.
east of Elliott Island,
Upper French River

George Turner's Bear Island site revealed only a barely discernible triangle and a few tally marks. He took us in his boat to another island site; but all we found was where it *had* been. The rocks that bore the paintings were gone. Thence we headed into the northwest arm of Timagami for one of the surprises of the summer.

I was puzzled when we turned in and landed at a nice camp site on the west shore; even more so when George climbed out, walked to a little cedar that grew close to the water's edge, got down on his hands and knees and peered through the branches. In a moment he turned back to us a grinning face, and beckoned. Thrusting my own face through the branches at water level, with one elbow in the water, I saw the Indian painting—on a little rock plane of a small boulder!

Voyageur Highway: East

On the voyageur route along the north shores of Lakes Superior and Huron and up the French River to Lake Nipissing one would expect to find a fair number of sites. To date I have recorded five, found another at Mica Bay that Keith Denis tracked down for me, and have got wind of two more.

Both the Killarney Bay site on Georgian Bay, and the Mica Bay one south of Agawa have a unique feature in common: the use of yellow and black along with the usual red. At both sites some symbols have a non-Indian look, especially those where black is involved. At Killarney white pigment has been mixed with both yellow and black.

The most tempting theory is to suppose that the voyageurs—especially those with Indian blood and beliefs —tried their hand at rock painting. Lumbermen may have, too; for at Willisville, just inland from Georgian Bay, there are tar paintings, clearly non-Indian, on Alligator Rock.

The Collins Bay site is in the conventional red again, on the rock-lined inner passage that the voyageurs used when Georgian Bay got too rough for comfort. Here is an animal head

94

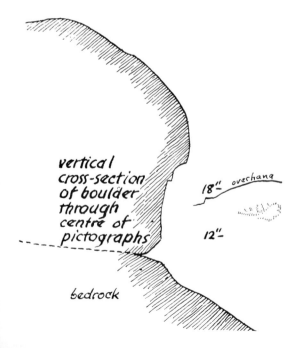

vertical cross-section of boulder through centre of pictographs

18" overhang

12"

bedrock

Northwest arm,
Lake Timagami

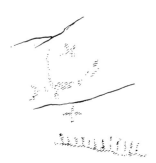

as bodiless as that on the Quetico Lake site. Here again is our ubiquitous—though somewhat battered—thunderbird, and tally marks, I should judge, rather than the alternative canoe.

Farther east, I had no success in finding "an astonishing serpent" referred to in Harmon's *Journal*, presumed to be in the vicinity of Grondines Point. In '59 I flew over the area, a complex labyrinth of small islands and shoals, all seeming to shelve gently into the water.

Eastward, the voyageurs ascended the French River to Lake Nipissing, crossed that lake, and portaged into the Ottawa watershed. In all that distance, so far, I have recorded only three sites and have yet to receive definite reports of any others. Site #33, just above Recollet Falls, faintly displays a small human figure and one other vague mark. Sites #79 and #80 were recorded through the hospitality—and original report—of John and Bill Kennedy. Both sites are at the upper end of the French River, not far west of Franks Bay on Lake Nipissing. The paintings on "Gibraltar," as it is called locally, are badly weathered, and little can be deciphered but a few canoes. Site #80, a bare half mile west of Keystone Lodge, is in clear, strong pigment. Only the thunderbird, turned on its side, is somewhat obscured by lichen. The stick figures remind us of those

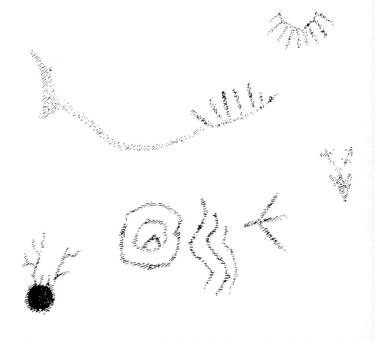

Site near
Killarney
Bay

at Diamond and Scotia Lakes. Among the others are a canoe, a pig-like bear, and a likely fish.

Southeast Ontario

Southward from Lake Nipissing the Shield formation reaches as far as the Severn River to the west, the Kawartha Lakes in the centre, and to the east breaks through the St. Lawrence Lowlands to form the Thousand Isles. In all this area only three pictograph sites have been recorded: one group of petroglyphs north of Stony Lake by Sweetman in 1955, and two rock painting sites, fifty miles east, on Lake Mazinaw. A survey of the lakes in this region would probably reveal an unsuspected proportion of raised water levels from lumbering operations that go back in some districts a full century and more. Lingering reports of rock paintings in the Muskoka–Parry Sound area so far have been impossible to localize. The one clear report I have is of paintings on a rock on the north shore of Lake Simcoe that broke off and fell into the water in 1914.

The Bon Echo site on Lake Mazinaw, however, amply compensates at least in extent for other sites that may have vanished in the area. The air view on the opposite page shows the *koo-chi-ching*, or "Little-lake-at-the-end-of-a-big-lake" of Lake Mazinaw, and the southern end of the main lake. The sandy spit we see is a part of the Bon Echo property, formerly owned by Merrill Dennison, now a Provincial Park. The huge granite escarpment on which the paintings appear is visible on the right, averaging 100 feet in height for a full mile. In numbers of paintings as well as for sheer bulk Bon Echo has no rival in Ontario. In June of '58 I recorded a hundred and thirty-

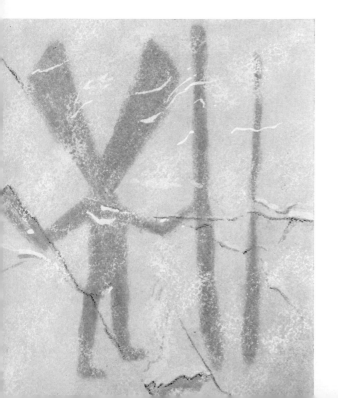

Lake Mazinaw
"Rabbit-man"

five symbols, scattered over twenty-seven faces.

Site #38, on Little Mazinaw, roughly a mile and a half south of the main site, has three faces.

The following pages illustrate only about a fifth of the actual paintings on the site, all easily accessible by canoe. Of those omitted many are either so weathered or so repetitive that the viewer would find them of minor interest. Handprints are entirely absent, canoes are rare, and the tendencies toward geometric types of abstractions so marked that we are tempted to ask whether the paintings are not the product of a culture quite distinct from those farther west. They seem older, too, in so far as a large number have been weathered to near-disappearance. There can be no reasonable doubt that the lake's present name (variously spelled in early references as "Massanog," "Massinaw," etc.) is from the Algonkian word for "picture," "writing," "painting," "book" (*mu-zi-nu-hi-gun*).

97

Lake Mazinaw, Face II

Site #99, south of Devil's Bay, Lake of the Woods

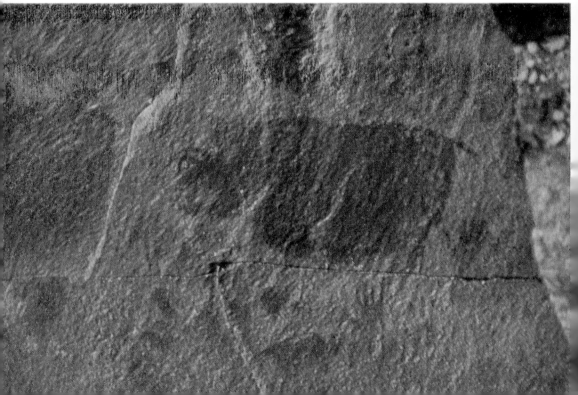

The colour reproduction on the opposite page is from Face II, the second most northerly, one of the strongest in colour, and as mystifying as any. The weird central figure is surely no native animal, although the shoulder-neck area is too badly weathered for the viewer to be able to make out the original outline. The strong suggestion of cloven hoofs is unique. Note the small animal beneath this one's belly—not identifiable either, but far more typical of the other animals on the site.

Even the canoe, if we so interpret the lower part of the painting, is strikingly different from others elsewhere. Are the diagonal strokes intended for arms, or paddles, or something else? And what about the strange little animal to the lower left (related perhaps to the large one), for dorsal spines are quite clear along its back, appearing also on the intact portion of the larger animal's back?

Below, by way of contrast, is a colour reproduction of the bison at Site # 99, on Lake of the Woods at the opposite end of the province.

When it comes to the human renderings above, we are again at a loss. Are these a hare's ears on this

99

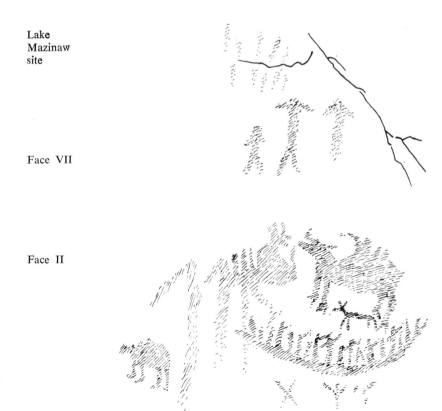

Lake
Mazinaw
site

Face VII

Face II

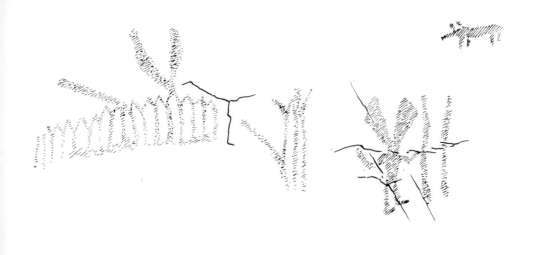

strange small figure? Or large feathers? If it is Ojibwa in origin we could make out a case for its representing *Nanabozho*, legendary hero and "demi-god," traditionally a hare. Among the northwestern Ojibwa he changes his name to *Wey-zuh-kay-chahk*, the Canada jay, or "Whiskey-jack."

Are other rabbit ears emerging from the "tectiform" to the left? This strangely structured form, unique to the Mazinaw site, appears again on two other faces.

Other figures on this page are not unlike some we have seen farther west. One is reminiscent of the mysterious Route Lake pair illustrated on page 67. The tiny figures at the bottom of the page suggest two "bird-men" in a canoe, and a turtle.

At the top left of the opposite page we have an abstraction which we are also tempted to relate to the "rabbit-man" already viewed. The face illustrated below it was most frustrating to record, much of it being too faint to trace directly. The rendering here suggests dorsal spines and a horned head, but these should be regarded

100

with some suspicion; I may well here have succumbed to my own wishful thinking. The more familiar forms below call for little comment, but those in the bottom margin are strange indeed. The one might have been influenced by a pottery design; the other might be described as "geometricized tree branches" for lack of a better guess.

On the next page are still further examples of relatively complex abstractions so typical of this site. Along with this tendency is an equally marked absence of any urge to naturalism, a trend that seems to grow in strength as one moves west. Recall that here we are on the southern periphery of the Shield formation and this is not too surprising. In historical times this was the border country between the nomadic Algonkian hunters of the Shield woodlands and the corn-raising Iroquoians of the St. Lawrence–Great Lakes lowlands. Regardless of the ebb and flow of prehistoric cultures, geography

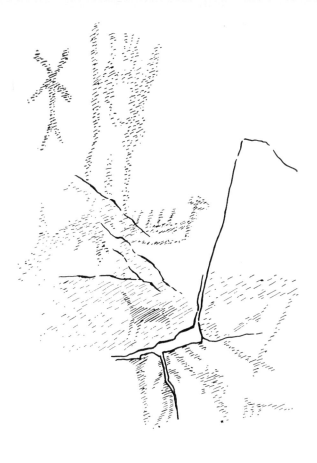

101

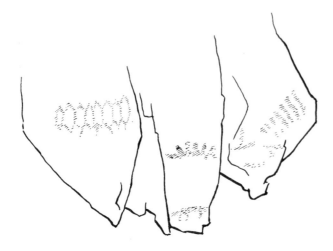

Site #37, Face XXVIIIa

Little Mazinaw Lake, Face III

would always have exerted a border-land influence here.

Beyond its geographical situation the Mazinaw setting itself must have exerted a powerful spell on any human group to whom it was familiar. The awe and disquietude associated with far less impressive sites in the north and west is clearly indicated by the lingering mythological associations. How much more would the Mazinaw setting have stimulated such responses!

For Christopher, Irene, and me it was a sobering experience merely to paddle along the base of this cliff, sensing the depth of the water beneath and the height of the rock above, where occasionally jutting crags eighty or ninety feet overhead seemed ready to plunge down on us —and undoubtedly *would* fall some day. One afternoon we were more than a little startled to see the water nearby begin an inexplicable whirling motion, accelerating till it lifted suddenly into a miniature waterspout, then vanishing as quickly as it had appeared. A trick of the air currents, no doubt, with thermals playing around the cliff on a hot summer day; but uncanny for all that.

Site #38 is only a mile south of the main Mazinaw site, with only three small faces, one of which is illustrated here. There surely were others in neighbouring lakes; but it is a century or more since lumbering operations began, and it is altogether likely that dams have drowned out the others. I have had only one report of another site, seen thirty years ago on Red Horse Lake in the Gananoque district. The report seems doubtful, however, for local people have no knowledge of this.

102

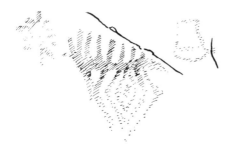

Site #37,
Face XXIV

The Search Continued

THE FIRST EDITION of this book was scarcely out when I began to wonder whether we might not have been hasty in publishing it, for reports of hitherto unknown sites kept trickling in. Meanwhile there was plenty of searching to do in the prairie provinces: for paintings in the foothills of Alberta and on sandstone outcroppings in the western coulees; for a whole cluster of petroglyph sites on the Milk River near the Montana border; for occasional glyphstones (small, carved boulders) scattered across the western prairie hill-tops; and for rock paintings in the Shield woodlands of northern Saskatchewan and Manitoba. Coming and going through Ontario, however, I chose my itinerary so as to pick up as many of the newly-reported sites in this province as possible. Finally, in 1965, the Quetico Foundation and Royal Ontario Museum supported a major effort to "clean up" the sites in the Ontario Shield woodlands. Now I have an adequate sampling of sites from the whole of the wooded Shield country as far northwest as the Hanging Ice River (south of Great Slave Lake), and southeastward through three provinces to the St. Lawrence River at Brockville, Ontario. Only Quebec and Newfoundland remain to be searched.

Year after year in Ontario, from the very beginning, the tally of newly-reported sites tended to total as high as the accumulation of recorded ones. It is impossible to name all the sources for these reports, but some must be mentioned. At the Lakehead Keith Denis has been an indefatigable detective from the first, and latterly Kenneth Dawson, now Professor of Anthropology at Lakehead University, has been passing on site locations. Nor may I pass over Jack Snider, *Times-Journal* columnist, whose beat is the whole of northwestern Ontario. But the greatest lift of all was an amazingly thorough and well-organized report from the District Office of the Department of Lands and Forests in Kenora by way of the Fish and Wild Life Division. Conservation Officer S. C. O. Linklater personally interviewed nearly every trapper in his district and took down verbatim descriptions of each site they knew of, including not only the pin-pointed locations but the number and type of paintings. I was astonished to find that he had listed fifty-seven sites in Kenora Forest District, nearly half of which I had never heard. For the first time, and in the heart of the pictograph country, I had a list of sites and locations I could have acquired in no other way. These were invaluable as a basis for estimating the distribution and density of sites throughout the Shield region.

Up until 1965 I had had only one chance to explore the northern periphery of the Shield in Ontario, and that had been plagued by bad flying weather. But a second chance opened up through the good offices of Lands and Forests and biologist Rod Standfield's wide-ranging beaver survey and polar bear count, which enabled me to reach three of the northernmost sites, as well as to interview Cree and Ojibwa residents as far north as Hudson Bay and as far east as James Bay.

To no one am I more indebted than to the old people—Cree, Ojibwa, and

Algonkin—whose straight talk and courtesy have given me many new insights into aboriginal modes of thinking, and into the ways in which these have been related to the rock paintings that they knew of. A number of these have since died, and it is more and more rarely now that I meet a man or woman whose memory reaches back beyond the turn of the century. Only a few of them passed on to the younger people what they could collect of old ways and beliefs. The old lore and practices are being submerged by the new, even as the flooding by lumber dams and hydro projects is drowning their forbears' paintings.

In the following pages I offer an account of the pictographs found in Ontario since the first edition of this book was published; pursuing for consistency's sake the same somewhat circuitous sequence of regions that was used under the section entitled "The Sites."

The Quetico-Superior Country

Through the observant eyes and proffered reports of Quetico Park portage crews, young canoe-trippers from Camp Owakonze, and scouts from the Moose Lake headquarters in Minnesota, the total of sites now located in Quetico Provincial Park has been doubled. Three more have been recorded on Darky, Kawnipi, and Kahshahpiwi Lakes. Six have been confirmed and pin-pointed, on Mackenzie, Doré, Ted, McAlpine, Cypress, and Shade lakes, and there are reports of others on Sturgeon, Cub, and Tuck lakes. Just beyond the

Park boundaries there are small sites on Iron Lake and Jordan Lake.

My first visit to Darky Lake illustrates how elusive a site may be. As my son Keewatin and I paddled down the east shore of Darky, and even after we found the first site, we scanned the opposite shore with binoculars to make sure we had missed nothing. So I was slightly doubtful in 1965 when I flew in from Nym Lake, even though I held a map on which a second site had been reliably pinpointed. Nor did it help, as the pilot circled for a landing, that I could see no rock where a rock should have been. It was not until we had come down, pulled off the canoe, and I had paddled—with almost complete scepticism—towards the marked place, that I caught a hint of dark rock through the trees, then rounded a point to stare at a 30-foot cliff, visible only from this angle. One human figure, a few handprints, and tally marks were all that were there, but a large mass of rock that might have borne other paintings had fallen away from below the human figure, and awaits the attention of an underwater archaeologist.

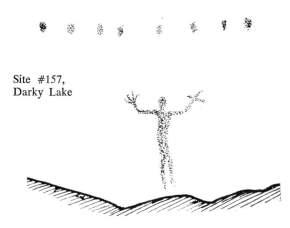

Site #157,
Darky Lake

Site #158, Kahshahpiwi Lake

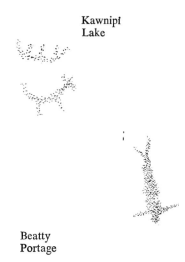

Beatty
Portage

That same summer my visit to a reported location on Kahshahpiwi Lake was somewhat thinly rewarded with the turtle and *sauromorph* shown here. The italicized word is the one I use to designate variations of the lizard-like abstractions found among the rock paintings from one end of the Shield woodlands to the other; the spots to either side of the head are not typical. Two years later an air search for a strayed canoe-tripper enabled me to be flown in to Kawnipi Lake where a small ambiguous animal and a canoe revealed themselves so faintly that I had to use Saran Wrap to trace them.

Regrettably there are still eight or nine sites in and near the Park that remain unrecorded. Yet only two or three of these, judging by the reports, amount to more than a single decipherable painting, and the seventeen sites that have been recorded comprise the most complete sampling I have obtained anywhere in the Shield country.

106

Border Lands West

It was only my early ineptness at interviewing, I realize now, that prevented me from learning the location of a site at the west end of Lac la Croix, near Beatty Portage on the Minnesota side of the lake, when I first visited Neguagon Reserve. For I cannot doubt that Charlie Ottertail knew where it was. This extraordinary old man, ill then, died a year later, taking with him most of what he knew about his people. My report of the site came from Professor T. D. Brock of Indiana University, along with colour slides that made its importance clear. The main group combines

Beatty
Portage

Beatty Portage, Site #156

three horned, semi-human figures in a mystifying relationship with a heavily antlered animal. I should qualify the word "horned" with the admission that I have jumped to unwarranted conclusions in assuming that the forked heads of two of these figures represent horns. Indeed, there seems to be a widespread "forked-head style," which I hesitate to designate as such before a serious study of style features and distributions has been made. The animals to the right of this group are too badly weathered to be identifiable, and most other material at this site is vestigial, excepting the intriguing form that one might take for a diving merman.

I had arranged an airlift in '66 to Sand Point Lake in Minnesota, not far south of Namakan Lake, but this had to be cancelled at the last minute. Reports of a site there suggest that it would be well worth a visit. I was luckier with a site north of Bear Pass on Rainy Lake, on Crowrock Inlet, now conveniently accessible by water

from the new Atikokan-Fort Frances highway. Many of the original paintings have been weathered beyond intelligibility against a background of dark, schistose rock. Extensive smearing or patination—it is difficult to know which—and the vague hints of frequent overpainting suggest that this was a long-used site. Lime deposits at the west end provide ideal contrast for the only clearly discernible group, whose "hubless wheel," associated tracks, and deer will immediately remind the reader of the Cuttle Lake paintings on page 72. The latter are only half a day's paddle northwest of Crowrock.

sprinkled with numerous small colonies of lichen

107

Crowrock

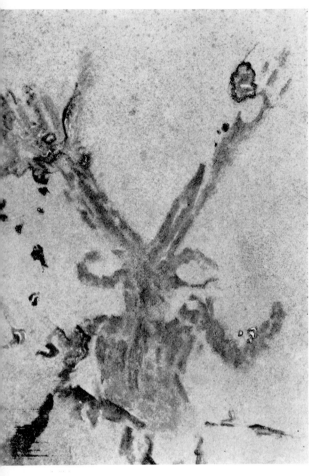

Northwest of Fort Frances and also accessible by road and outboard is a granite formation on Burditt (or Clearwater) Lake where the paintings are so severely weathered and overpainting has so clearly occurred that I am sure some of the paintings are of quite early origin. The unique feature is the quasi-human form reproduced here. I would guess that the upper projections from the head, made by dragging the paint outwards with four fingers, were intended to represent supernatural power emanating from a shaman's mind. The lower circular projections may possibly be ears; but on no other Shield painting have I found human ears represented.

The water route out of Burditt brings one through a wild rice lake and on to Footprint Lake, out of which a short, easy portage passes over into Jackfish Lake. Where this portage climbs over a hump of bedrock I found the answer to a question that had plagued me for eight years, ending a hope I had had, but demonstrating what tricks the mind can play with its own memories and observations. In 1957, a Fort Frances informant told me about the tracks of a man and a dog in the living rock, and others said they had heard of these. But no one could locate the place. I did not take the report too seriously until two years later when Peter and I found petroglyphs carved in a reef in Sunset Channel on Lake of the Woods. The commercial fisherman who pin-pointed the site said he had seen "moose tracks" there. ("Painted on the rock," his wife said, but he contradicted her.) That same sum-

Burditt Lake,
Site #196

mer, talking to the people on Northwest Bay Reserve, I was told of a man's and a moose's tracks on the portage out of Footprint Lake. What an idiot I had been! Man and moose, or man and dog, this was surely a petroglyph site! Arriving there at last I soon found the "footprints." Alas, there was only one of each, and both were obviously caused by the weathering out of pockets of softer rock, requiring in either case a high degree of wishful thinking to be interpreted as anything else.

But wishes die hard. A case in point is a Minnesota correspondent who sent me his photographs of a single giant human footprint in solid Precambrian rock, along with the complaint that his photographs were totally unsatisfactory for reasons he could not understand. A glance sufficed to make it clear that the "footprint" was the result of natural erosion. But how does one convince a person against his will that what the physical eye beholds may differ radically from what the mind's eye projects? Indeed, in comparing photographs of the cave paintings in southwestern Europe with the seemingly meticulous copies by dedicated scientists one is uneasily aware of many subtle projections which stray from a strictly objective rendering. But the camera has its strict limitations too, and in my opinion there is no adequate substitute for a study of the original painting, *in situ*.

South of Footprint, a mere stone's throw from the Ojibwa settlement at Northwest Bay, is a rock so smeared with pigment that I was tempted to designate it as a site. This, and a paint-smeared rock on Eagle Lake, are the only instances of smearing unaccompanied by at least a handprint or two. At Northwest Bay I was told that the paint had "always been there."

Jackfish paintings, Site #195

109

Petroglyphs,
Lake of the Woods

Photograph by Peter Dewdney

Lake of the Woods

To the thirteen sites previously recorded in or near the Lake of the Woods another five have been added; three on the lake itself, and two on Silver Lake, a short drive north of Kenora. Thanks to Mickey Linklater I was also able to add four more petroglyph sites, making a cluster of six such occurrences in the northwest part of the lake, all on horizontal shelves of chlorite schist. A sample glyph is shown here. The contrast was provided by rubbing chalk over the surrounding surface rather than following the questionable practice of filling in the grooves.

Highway 71, on its way from Fort Frances to Kenora, touches a long, crooked arm of Sabaskong Bay at Nestor Falls, on the shores of which two small but interesting sites occur. In the one case only the finger draggings out of a smeared area qualify it as a pictograph site; but they are associated with a low, shallow cave where a large lens of rock softer than the prevailing dark, schistose one has been weathered out. Less than two miles north of this a smooth-faced hump of granite rises steeply from the shore. A small break in the formation forms a protected setting for paintings on either side of an angular rock. On the left are two likely bears—regardless of the long ears on the one—and their tracks, and to the right are canoes and tally marks. Bears and bear tracks appear frequently on the Miday scrolls, but never in this kind of configuration. I would judge that both groups were by the same hand.

There remain unrecorded a number of small sites to the east of Nestor Falls, notably in Crow Portage Bay, and on Stephen, Pinus, Barry, and Kakagi lakes.

Sabaskong
Bay, Site #198

Silver Lake,
Site #224

-4"

diagonal
streaks due
to glacial grooving

-72"

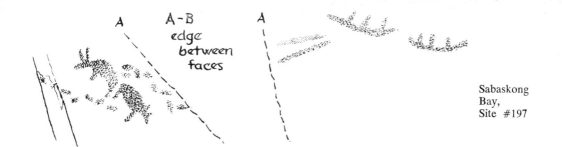

A-B
edge
between
faces

Westward from here, Chris and I found one faint painting of a snake on the north shore of Obabikon Lake within the Aulneau Peninsula of Lake of the Woods. Thence, we flew westward over the north end of the Great Traverse, briefly viewing historic Massacre Island where some two and a half centuries earlier La Vérendrye's nephew and men were wiped out by Siouan raiders. At Northwest Angle I hoped to get more specific information about a site reported in the area, but no one there then knew of it and a brief air search of the nearby swamp and muskeg revealed no hint of a water-facing rock outcrop.

A day later Chris and I drove out to Silver Lake where we launched the canoe to explore the large island off the north shore. Although I had had several reports of a site there, all had been so vague that I expected very little. In a sense I was right, for the only clear figure was the one repro-duced here, a very abstract animal. But it turned out that there were actually two sites, with handprints, tally marks, and extensive smearing, some of them obscured by extensive growths of Caloplaca—more fashionably known nowadays as Xanthoria—the brilliant and ubiquitous orange-hued lichen, which seems to prefer rocks of sedimentary derivation.

Besides the site off Northwest Angle Bay that we couldn't locate, there remain half a dozen unrecorded Lake of the Woods sites, including two or three in the water maze known as Whitefish Bay. There remains, too, the intriguing mystery of the site offerings (p. 154). Latterly I have heard that "prayer sticks" are hung from trees back in the bush as well as below rock paintings, and that their function is to revive the "power" of a shaman, but I have yet to find anyone who can speak with authority on the subject.

Stephen Lake
Photograph by L. Compton

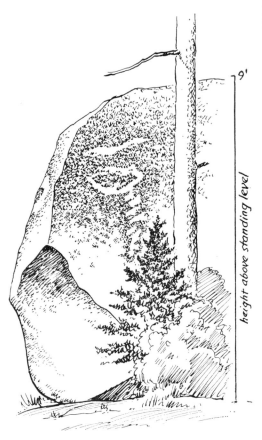

height above standing level

9'

Northwestern Hinterland

To find the northwesternmost rock paintings known in the province we must fly nearly four hundred miles due north of Kenora to a small rock outcrop well beyond the discernible edge of the Shield. This rock briefly borders the muddy and treacherous Sachigo River, which experienced bush pilots prefer to avoid. I got there in the fall of '65 on a Beaver transect with Rod Standfield, the aircraft too heavily laden with extra gas drums to be able to carry a canoe. Pilot Al

Bieck gave the river a long and thorough inspection—although we knew this was one of the few places where aircraft did land—before he brought us down. Then he manoeuvred the Beaver with consummate skill against the conflicting thrusts of a brisk wind and a strong current while I hung out on the wing strut sketching and photographing the faint paintings that I could just discern at 30 feet from the rock. What is reproduced here is accurate as far as it goes, but there may have been other paintings too faint to show at that distance. At Cross Lake in adjacent Manitoba I heard of another site on the Sachigo, but my informant was almost blind and could not pin-point it on the map for me.

On another transect I was dropped off at Bearskin Lake, west of Big Trout, to check the report of a site that I had failed to find on my only other excursion so far north. An Ojibwa fisherman took me in his kicker down a small stream to Nighthawk Rapids on the Severn River where the rough indication of a nighthawk had been scraped from the rock tripe that covered the upper part of a ten-ton boulder just above the rapids. The local story goes that the nighthawk tried to imitate the noise of the rapids, which so offended the Manitou of the place that he converted the bird's head into this boulder.

All along the northern fringe of the Shield woodland—as far west as Lake Athabaska—I have heard of "writings" or "carvings" which failed to materialize on investigation. These can be explained as lichen glyphs, the memory and rumours of which have

112

Sachigo River,
Site #246

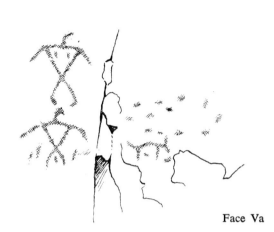

Face IV

lingered long after the scraped areas had grown in. It was clear that the Nighthawk site had been re-scraped at intervals, but secretly, for I got the usual opinion that it had always been there. I doubt if this will continue long. Early in this century an Anglican Cree catechist from York Factory by the name of William Dick travelled from one band to another as far east as James Bay, converting the great majority to Christianity with astounding and apparently permanent success so that there is actually less knowledge of aboriginal beliefs and practices in these remote areas than there is beside the railway tracks in the south. Only some vague notions of the Maymaygayshi, and the unquenchable, bawdy Weysakaychauk stories persist.

Farther south, yet in a region where both rocks and people are still spread thin, it was a surprise to find a major group of paintings on the Donnelly River, just south of North Caribou Lake, with a smaller site less than a mile away. On both sites the paintings appear at the foot of modest rock walls, on faces that have been kept clear of lichen by wave wash and periodic flooding. At the top of the page are a faint moose, a hornless deer (note the feet, split to show the hooves), two thunderbirds, and sundry indecipherables. Much of what is illustrated below is badly weathered, but

Face Va

a variation of the female symbol is discernible, and among the faint figures in the main group one can make out a headless man, one and perhaps two thunderbirds, and a quasi-human figure. A special interest attaches to the animal enclosed in an oval, which I guess to have been intended for a bear either in hibernation or in a snare. Above the crack is a vague thunderbird and some vestigial material that is even more vague in the original. The second site on the Donnelly consists mainly of badly weathered tally marks, and is not illustrated here.

Face VIII

East of these sites, near the west end of Wunnumin Lake, there seems to be a small site which I have not yet been able to pin-point; and there is a reliable report of one on the Asheweig River a mere thirty air miles south of Big Trout.

Swinging west to Big Sandy Lake we come to the one area of the western Shield woodlands where my sampling may prove to have been inadequate, although one vague location to the northwest and a pin-pointed one just south of that large lake are all that I have in my files. South of Sandy we reach Deer Lake and the northern edge of a concentration of sites that straddles the Ontario-Manitoba boundary between the trapping community of Little Grand Rapids and the mining one of Red Lake, in Ontario.

The Ojibwa in this region have kept their old practices and beliefs to an unusual degree. For example, in 1946, a Little Grand Rapids trapper bought a trapping charm, which he claims is still effective, from a shaman in Red Lake for $385. No doubt it is, for the ritual required in the use of this little leather bag and its undisclosed contents ensures among other things that its owner will visit every trap and snare on his line with un-failing and frequent regularity. And he *is* reputed to be the best trapper working out of Little Grand Rapids.

North of Deer Lake is the Cochrane River site already described on page 59. On the lake itself, is a group of paintings recorded by Professor Kidd in McIntosh Bay. Here, the rendering of an animal among a number of weathered abstractions is locally identified as a rabbit, its state of preservation suggesting a more recent origin than the others. If the reader is dubious about the importance of this inoffensive little animal he will be reassured to learn that the bite of a rabbit is widely believed to confer a long life on the lucky recipient. There are other paintings a mere air-hop south on Hanging Lake, quite as badly weathered as their reproduction here shows.

This brings us, still moving south, into the drainage basin of the Berens River along which, on the Manitoba side, I recorded three groups of paintings in 1966. Another remains unrecorded, but on the Ontario side there are still at least eight unvisited sites, six of them reliably pin-pointed at Child's Falls, on Stout, Shibumeni, Pikanjikum, and Hornblendite lakes, and near Poplar Hill. The name of another lake, Mamakwash, is ob-

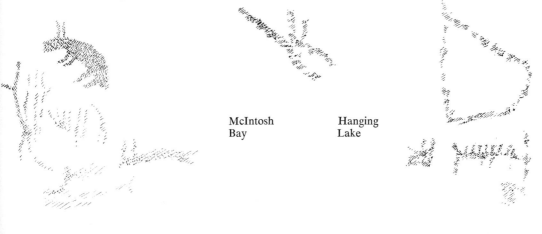

McIntosh
Bay

Hanging
Lake

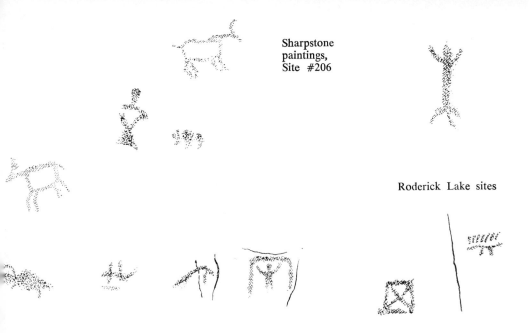

Sharpstone paintings, Site #206

Roderick Lake sites

viously a variant spelling of Maymaygwayshi, but when I flew over it in 1965 there were few indications of rock outcrops so the site reported there is likely to be a very small one.

On the east of the water complex called Sharpstone and Stout lakes there are at least seven sites, three of which I have recorded. One of these has already been discussed in this book, and another is illustrated here, including a tiny but unmistakable bear, and an hour-glass style of figure —a type that is rarely found so far north.

Two southern tributaries of the Berens River are the Dogskin and the Keeper, the latter named from a family widely known for its shamanistic skills. In the Keeper system are Roderick and Herod Lakes. Paintings from just west of Herod Lake are shown here. Four small figures are scattered along eleven feet of rock only a few inches above the 1964 water level, and in the high water of 1966 I should never have found them. Note the framed human figure, the enclosing line perhaps representing the *waubik*, or place, where the Maymaygwayshi lives. Most informants in this area assert that the mysterious rock dweller is no taller than a child and has no nose.

When Jake Siegel and I were paddling back to the Beaver after recording the single otter-like figure which was all we had found on the reported site on Roderick Lake, we met an Ojibwa and family who were netting trout. I had barely told him what I was doing than he was leading us to the two modest little abstractions, reproduced here, situated close to the water in a little narrows less than two miles away.

115

Two years later, back with Jake again, we landed near the mouth of a sluggish stream flowing into Frances Lake on the Dogskin River only a few miles from the Manitoba boundary. We had been encountering a succession of unexciting petrographs so we should have been prepared for the surprise. On a glacially polished granite face 10 feet above the water, deeply patinated by long exposure and heavily limed by calcite-bearing seepage, was the find of the summer. The four human figures here, I am sure, though I cannot yet prove it, are among the oldest I have recorded anywhere. Unfortunately we have as yet few clues as to how old is "old." The glacially smoothed surface of the rock at the Frances Lake site tells us that it has endured since the last ice retreat virtually unchanged except for a thin coating of deposited lime. This was precipitated on the rock not only before and after the paintings were made, but apparently before they had time to bond to the rock for the seepage seems to have converted some of the anhydrous red oxide into the hydrous yellow one, staining the surrounding area with a strong yellow ochre tint. The setting has always been well protected from the weather and the lime-bearing seepage as well as the absence of other moisture has inhibited lichen growth. Yet lichens have managed to establish themselves and have begun to encroach on the paintings. Finally, the style and content suggest an early origin for the paintings. Only one other site, a mere twenty-five miles north, just inside Manitoba and east of Fishing Lake, shows similar features. As here, the

Frances Lake, Site #208, sole face

human figures, although clearly the work of another hand, have tail-like appendages. Both groups show bows and arrows.

In the Milk River glyphs, male genitals are frequently included in human figures, but in the Shield paintings they are rare. If these "tails" were intended for phallic renderings we have a clear exception to the general practice, which could be the survival of an earlier style that has disappeared from the more exposed sites. I believe that the representation of bows and arrows adds to the case for an early origin. We may surmise, from the few sites where guns are painted, that the shaman's preference was for the more prestigious weapon. Even in the stage when early firearms were inferior to the rapidly re-strung bow, the noise and flame they pro- duced gave them a supernatural aspect; and news of this awesome weapon travelled far inland long be- fore its actual appearance. I contend that the bows and arrows here were painted before the contact period, and the settings of these two sites emphatically support the contention.

Unique, and most intriguing is the figure at the upper left. Jake and I both felt that this fantastic apparition should have a second wing, but could find no trace of colour where it should have been. The treatment of this creature's feet is extremely curious. The curves of the toes seem to have run away with the artist, as if they had exerted an hypnotic influence to the point where his interest had been transferred from the intended form to the fascination of developing a fantastic one.

117

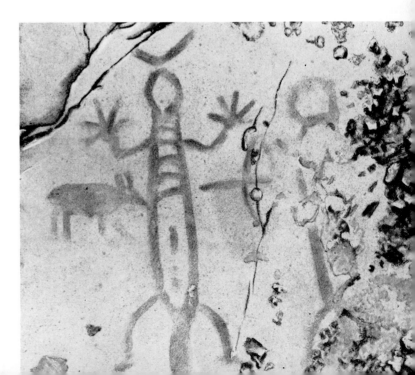

Face Ia

Face III

To continue our sweep southward along the Manitoba boundary we come to the Bloodvein River system. Within an area comparable to that of Quetico Provincial Park there is a matching density of sites, with seven known locations on the Manitoba side and nine in Ontario. Hansen Lake (east of Rostoul), Bigshell, and Beamish lakes all add their water to the upper Bloodvein, while Larus and Artery lakes are enlargements of the mainstream. The dramatic site just east of Artery has already been described on page 60. About thirty-five miles upstream just west of Larus Lake is a group of paintings in a similar setting. Both sites have a northerly exposure. This would normally ensure a heavy growth of lichens because of the lack of sunlight that would speed the drying of the surface after a wind-driven rain. On both these sites, however, the granite has been so smoothed by glacial action that the algae and fungus spores, whose union makes the plant possible, find little encouragement to lodge on any rock faces that are also protected by overhangs. The upper portion of the second face of the Larus-Bloodvein site, consisting of vestigial handprints and abstractions, is not shown here, and much that is illustrated is familiar enough from other sites that the reader will require no comment. My rendering of the human figure at the base of Face III reflects my uncertainty as to whether the apparent head-dress, and detail attached to the body actually belong to the original. What is both striking and clear, though the colour is faint, is the large figure holding up the

Various faces of the
Larus-Bloodvein Site #154

Face IIa

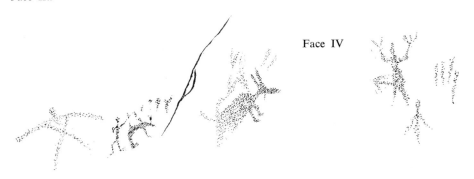

Face IV

smaller one: a sort of giant-and-pygmy motif. Nothing more readily invites the viewer's personal projections: Is it a father proudly displaying his new-born son? Or a Weyndigow about to devour his human victim?

Regarding handprints, I might note that I know of only one occurrence farther west, on a site near Snow Lake, northeast of The Pas, Manitoba. Southward they abound to the Shield's edge, but to the east they extend only a site or two past Lake Nipigon.

The second set of Larus-Bloodvein paintings is even more obscured than the reproductions on this page suggest. The alert viewer will pick out five human figures, if he includes the one in a thunderbird style and the tiny little human beside a vaguely animal form. The animal with the heavy shoulder hump and the long ears—against a background of vestigial paintings—I take for a moose, mainly because a bell is faintly visible.

119

Of the other Bloodvein sites, the one on Hansen Lake is the most interesting. The setting, reproduced in colour on page 131, illustrates how some granite formations will break so neatly as to give the setting an artificial aspect. The patination of one face is so strong that it can easily be spotted from the air. Geologists are naturally reluctant, without seeing the rock itself, to make any pronouncements about the reasons for this ruddy patination except to say that sun and rain acting on microscopic particles of iron in the rock could oxidize them into the anhydrous red compound. For me the colour associates with long exposure, the more so because on the sandstone cliffs of the Milk River in Alberta there is a clear correlation between age and patination. The question arises whether the aboriginal artist was attracted to the ruddier faces because of colour already there, or whether the colour might possibly be due to a long succession of paintings, made over the centuries, whose form had weathered out, but whose residual colour had accumulated to achieve this general ruddiness. All such speculations must remain merely that until a microscopic examination is made of actual rock samples.

Note the faint human figure above the deer-like animal on the far right face. Of greater interest is the third group from the left where a man is holding a line (of supernatural power, or merely a rawhide snare?) that partly encircles the animal. Here I yield to the temptation to throw scientific caution to the winds, allowing myself to imagine a shaman's dream in which he has snared the Source Animal, the Sacred Caribou, who yields him the power to be a great caribou-hunter. Or perhaps he awoke with the knowledge of how to construct a caribou-hunting charm.

The remaining sites in the Blood-

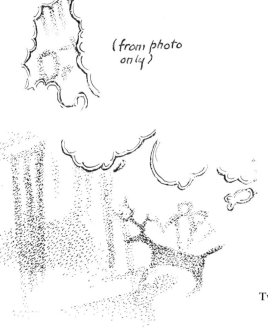

(from photo only)

Two faces of the Hansen Lake Site #215

vein country east of Manitoba are all slight, calling for few comments. The moose shown here is the sole painting on Musclow Lake. Larger than the usual style, it is nevertheless small compared with two others in Manitoba, one of which, near the mouth of the Bloodvein, is nearly half life-size. At Beamish there is only one small snakish form, and at Bigshell only a single little animal, drawn as if it were falling from beneath the deep overhang. I do not know what to make of the vague "half-wheel" reproduced here from a site on the north arm of Artery Lake; but I was startled to find a small black sauromorph nearby, the only black painting I know of in the Shield that is clearly aboriginal.

On a small, unnamed lake just to the west of Barclay—another enlargement of the Bloodvein—is a single figure with a phallic appendage. A vicious-looking electrical storm was threatening as Jake took me down to the water, too imminent to give us time to unstrap the canoe. Fortunately the painting was large and clear enough for me to sketch and photograph from the wing strut as Jake taxied past. As we swung around for the fourth run the sky went black. I scrambled into the plane, Jake opened the throttle, and I made my last-second corrections through the window as we roared past on the take-off. We raced the storm all the way back to the Red Lake base, where we were still roping the Beaver to her moorings as the first fierce gusts lashed the waves into white-caps and a grey wall of rain closed in.

South of the upper Bloodvein complex of lakes and streams is the region drained by the Winnipeg River and its main branch, the English. In the course of hydro development two sites, on Umfreville and Oneman lakes, have been flooded, but another, on the English north of Maynard Lake, is still above water. Eight other small sites in this general area remain on my list of unrecorded ones: on Roger, Fletcher, Huston, Flintstone, Haggart, Jadel, and Rex lakes, and on the Muskeg River. By 1961, however, I had got a reasonable sampling from the region with one elusive exception.

Musclow Lake

North arm of Artery Lake

deep overhang

Beamish Lake

Face II in black pigment

Three years earlier I had received an enthusiastic report to the effect that there were more than a hundred paintings "near the portage" at the south end of Sydney Lake. On the strength of this, although I hadn't interviewed the original informant, I flew in from Kenora with a young photographer from Atikokan, Klaus Prufer, prepared for a four-day sojourn that would allow ample time for a thorough job on even so large a site. We pitched our camp and set out for the site. By the fourth day we had scanned every rock outcrop in the lake and south of it within a twenty mile radius of our base, exploring a full eighty miles of shorelines, to find exactly nothing! Our only dividend was the few hours I took off on the fourth morning to study lichen occurrences on a magnificent series of granite cliffs to learn how these related to weather exposure, drip, seepage, sunlight, and so on.

I never found this mythical site, the report of which might have been based on two other sites reported later on nearby Pine Needle Lake. The latter report was so clear and seemingly reliable that I had no hesitation in marking the locations on the map I handed to Jake as we set out one afternoon on my last trip of the season out of his base. Our first view of the lake reinforced my confidence, for a whole succession of high rocks lined the north shore where the sites were marked. The formation fell away to the west, but reappeared briefly on the north shore of the "couchiching," Ojibwa for "a little lake at the end of a big lake." We dropped down at the east end and began taxiing past the cliffs, scanning them one by one for the first sign of colour that would be our signal for taking off the canoe. At the end of the run we had seen exactly nothing. We taxied back, fruitlessly, although wind conditions were such that we could approach the rocks at near wing-tip distance.

There was only one possible conclusion—another wild goose chase! Reluctantly we took off, and it didn't help my mood as we circled for altitude to see the broad expanse of Sydney Lake gleaming on the horizon. My eyes returned to the Pine Needle cliffs, scanning and scanning as if I could see from a thousand feet what had not shown up at thirty. I glanced, too, at the small outcrop on the shore of the couchiching, thinking I really should have had a look at it, and then decided I had had enough disappointments for one day. I nudged Jake, however, and pointed it out to him. "Want to take a look?" he asked. I shook my head decisively. "Let's go home." He banked the plane to head for Red Lake, while I stared down at the little rock on the couchiching. Then I touched Jake's arm again. "Let's go down!"

He made one of his beautifully precise landings to bring us alongside a convenient dead spruce that projected out into the water making a convenient dock right beside the rock. I had only to open the door to see colour on the nearest face. From the float I could see the paintings. Lots of them! Later Jake claimed that I behaved like a maniac, but even on his habitually impassive countenance there broke out the broadest and happiest smile I had ever seen on it.

Nor had I ever seen so individual a site. Almost every painting was unlike any I had recorded elsewhere. Most unique of all was the strange, insect-like form in the centre. But the decorated ovals, the vertical patterns above, and the hand-forms extended into "gauntlets" were all equally unusual. Then I noticed some peculiar markings, too consistently parallel to be separate tally marks, and requiring for their execution some sort of comb-like tool. In one instance this could only have been rotated to achieve the curved, parallel lines that were there. Four years later and a two-day canoe trip farther west I was to find in Manitoba a cluster of markings that I am convinced were made by the identical tool.

Were these mere doodles? This is no idle question. For doodling in its purest form is automatic writing: the hand draws at the behest of the unconscious while the conscious mind is blank or focussed on other matters. It may be, indeed, that many of the Shield paintings were made in a trance-like state, so that the shaman who made them might later view the forms with wonder and awe, believing that a supernatural hand had produced them.

The only other painting here that calls for a comment is the quasi-human figure with the trifurcated crown. It is rarely that any detail is added to a human head other than horns or the forked effect that may be a variant power symbol. I should add that I returned to Pine Needle the following summer, where Jake left me to scan every inch of the rock on the main lake from my canoe. The sole result was the single faint little figure, broken off at the base, that is shown here.

East of Red Lake and north of Lac Seul I found two sites not previously recorded. The one on Picture Paint Lake displays only a few smearings and vestigial abstractions. The other, on Bluffy Lake, includes a turtle, a partly disfigured deer, and

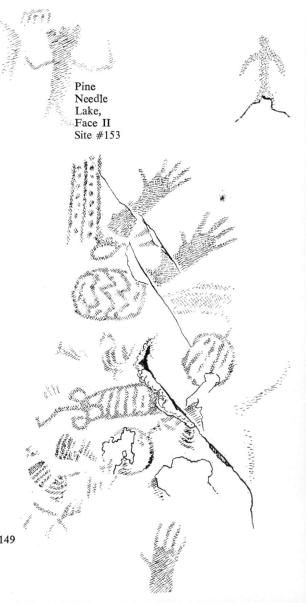

Pine
Needle
Lake,
Face II
Site #153

Main face of
major Pine
Needle Site #149

Bluffy
Lake

two tally marks. There was likely more, but some misguided person had disfigured the face with red paint, and lichen encroachment obscured the rest. Only the turtle is reproduced here.

Still farther east I was able to taxi close enough to a small site on Lake St. Joseph, a few miles west of abandoned Osnaburgh House, to confirm a site reported there, but had no canoe from which to record it. Downstream, the Albany River that drains Lake St. Joseph widens into Petewanga Lake, and there is a single small group of paintings there of which I have two records: a drawing by McInnes in 1904, which I found in one of his notebooks, and a

Sample from McInnes' field notes
Courtesy, Geological Survey of Canada

photograph taken only a few years ago, which I got from Roscoe Richardson. I would guess that this represents a Maymaygwayshi, and that the tally marks record the number of times the painter dreamed his access into the rock. I have a report of another site "on the Wabassi River, near Fort Hope, about two days' travel from its source," but have not yet been able to get to Fort Hope to confirm or pin-point it.

In the whole of the northwestern region there remain twenty-eight sites I know of that are still unrecorded; no doubt there are as many more, some of which may forever go unnoticed. But I am reasonably sure that none of these is a major site, and those now recorded offer a fair sampling of the total.

The West-Central Hinterland

Within the roughly rectangular region that is bounded by Lake of the Woods, Lac Seul, Lake Nipigon, and Quetico Provincial Park the frequent outcroppings of granite and the lavish distribution of lakes provide numerous settings for rock art, so that even

124

Beetle(?)
Dryberry Lake

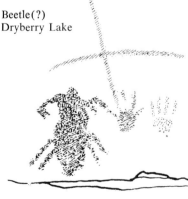

Photograph by L. Compton

as of this writing new reports keep turning up.

Peter and I had already recorded two sites in the north end of Dryberry Lake when I got wind of two more: paintings at the lake's southwest outlet, and possible glyphs on the west shore. The day on which I recorded the paintings was too rough and gusty for a landing on the west shore so the glyphs remain uninvestigated, but the paintings alone fully justified the trip. Part of the setting forms a natural outdoor picture gallery, even to the square ledge of rock at just the right height for docking a boat. Farther along the shore the paintings are scattered at intervals only a foot or two above the prevailing water level.

The upper paintings of the first group contained only one surprise; the suggestion of a bird's wing with feathers exaggerated into long, rhythmic curves, but no hint of a second wing excepting the line that might have been its upper edge extending leftward into the obscure abstractions there. The rosy patination of the background again raises the possibility of earlier paintings, and this suggestion of age is reinforced by the variety of styles as well as the various states of preservation. At least six different artists worked here. Note— just under the strong and rather crudely painted monster with the big tail—a delicate drawing of a human figure. The details on this are much too fine for a finger painting, unless single strokes had been made with a small lump of red ochre retraced once with a wet finger. Two other human figures can be distinguished if we include the one with a head like a vacuum tube. The striking figure off by itself near the waterline reminds me vaguely of the large water beetle that will sometimes dart from one dark rock to another under the water at a site. Yet Algonkian mythologists seem to have had little interest in the insect world.

Face I

Site #186,
Dryberry Lake

Face II

Face III

The canoe route out of the northeast end of Dryberry brings the traveller over a short portage into the Wabigoon-English drainage by way of Teggau and Eagle lakes. I have yet to visit a small site south of Teggau, the existence of which I was unaware when I recorded the two sites on that lake. The settings for both are magnificent; sheer granite cliffs rear a hundred feet above the water, alternately streaked with contrasting passages of orange-hued Xanthoria lichen, the jet black seepage-fed varieties, and the vivid white of precipitated lime, all vertically patterned by gravity. Here and there on the occasional brief corridor of bare rock, the aborigines' paintings appear. The paintings shown to the lower right were made from an easily accessible ledge 10 feet above the water. The only one that calls for comment is the domino-like arrangement of eight spots, perhaps intended to indicate as many days.

The second Teggau site contains no discernible drawings, and only a few handprints and finger draggings. But the extent and effect of the smeared passages are impressive. On other sites a slight case may be made for the notion that smearing practices meant nothing more than a desire on the part of the artist to rub the paint off his hands. Here, however, the smearing extends over such large areas that far more red ochre than was normally available to any individual would have been needed even to cover the smaller faces, and in one instance the smearing extends 14 feet above the water to a height where it would need to have been

applied with a paint-soaked hide or bundle of sphagnum lashed to the end of a pole. Possibly a large group contributed their paint supplies for a ritual by the cliffside, the nature of which we can only guess.

Lesser smearings are found as far to the northwest as Tramping Lake in Manitoba, but I can recall having found none east of Lake Nipigon. Here, at Teggau Lake, seems to have been the centre of the whole region in which smearing occurs. Whether it originated and spread from this locale, or merely reached its climax here is not known.

126

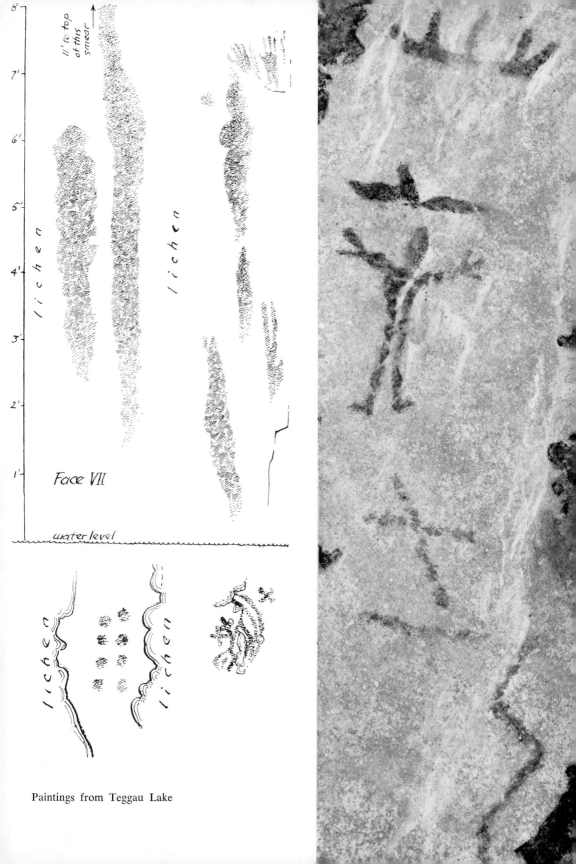

8'

11' to top
of this
smear

7'

6'

5'

lichen

4'

lichen

3'

2'

1'

Face VII

water level

lichen

lichen

Paintings from Teggau Lake

Not far east of Teggau, two sites have been reported on Delano Lake, just south of Eagle Lake. On Osbourne Bay one site has been noted, and to the east there are unrecorded occurrences on Ingolf and Doré lakes. Canyon Lake, northwest of Eagle, has yielded no reports in spite of its name, but on nearby Shrub Lake there is a single painting of a "very bright" moose; and where the Canyon River empties into the Wabigoon west of Clay Lake there is a site I have heard of from three separate sources. Northward again, my friend Jack Snider reports a fourth site at Route Lake, unsuspected when we visited the place in 1960.

On Highway 17 east of Eagle Lake is the town of Dryden, redolent when the wind is wrong with the fumes of kraft paper in the making. A short drive north is Kaiashkomin (Gullwing) Lake, at the northeast end of which is an interesting little collection of paintings. Shown here are a weird abstracted animal form and a deerlike animal, which for some reason, perhaps connected with the encircling line, is tilted backward from a normal position. At the opposite end of the lake a second site had been reported, and though I found no paintings there I did find a niche where tobacco offerings are still being deposited, the most recent a cellophane-wrapped cigar!

Face I,
#194

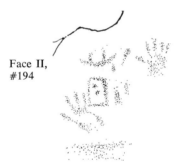

Face II,
#194

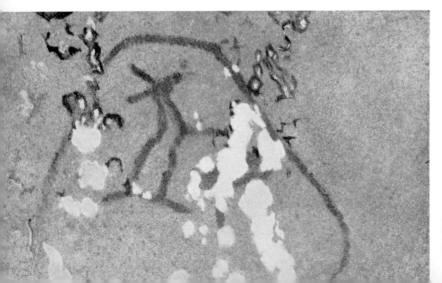

Face III,
Kaiashkomin Lake,
Site #194

Face III

Basket Lake,
Site #222

Face I

Paintings at
Abamatagwia Lake

We circled around the hinterland area between Eagle and Rainy lakes that centres on Lower Manitou, where there are paintings that have already been described (p. 74). Two other sites have turned up only a brief air-hop to the west, one on suggestively-named Picture Narrows Lake, the other on adjoining Penassi. East of Manitou, between Vickers and Dogfly, is a single painting of a canoe, and from Vickers itself a group of half a dozen figures has been reported. Other sites farther east, on Smirch and Kinnyu lakes, have not yet been pin-pointed.

North of Highway 17 the sites thicken. To the west are Mameigwess and Indian lakes, sites already familiar to the reader. Only a little farther west I found paintings—shown here —on Abamatagwia and Basket lakes. Notable on Basket Lake (more properly "Fishtrap," I was told locally) is the peculiar moose-like creature, its tail and stack extended to meet so that they form a box which also serves for the animal's body. The two rather peculiar forms on an adjoining face mystified me until I saw McInnes' sketch, in which the two were joined in a single serpentine form.

Near the narrows on Abamatagwia a great tilted block of granite thrusts into the water, making an awkward but quite possible place to stand as long as the rock is dry. In my case there was a surfeit of tent caterpillars that threatened to grease the slope if stepped on, and I had to brush them off ahead of me as I worked my way up to the paintings. In spite of the protective over-hang five species of lichen encroach on the main face, obscuring a few of the paintings, which vary from sauromorphs to distinctly human figures.

Until the Turbo-Beaver came into service Ignace was the Lands and Forests' air base for servicing the greater part of the hinterland we are concerned with here. Ignace's veteran Chief Ranger is Fred Nicholls, whose experience goes back to the days of the Ontario Forestry Branch, when rangers paddled to their fires by canoe, and fought them with a pack-pump. Fred recalls, too, the days when the local Ojibwa still practised tent-shaking. Here, single-handed, Conservation Officer Von Rosen has tracked down six pictograph locations in his district. Four of these six lie within an area of less than a thousand square miles north and east of Ignace, within which four others have been reported by D. P. Rogers of the Ontario Department of Mines. out over a footing that slopes steeply

This brings us to White Otter Lake directly south of Ignace, on whose shores stands the amazing log edifice built by the Old Country swain whose girl told him she wouldn't marry him until he built her a castle. The "castle" is there, but the girl never came. On the east side of Ann Bay imposing cliffs handsomely streaked with lichens and lime stand just north of a beautiful sand beach. Through a comedy of errors, including the loan by its absent-minded owner of an outboard motor with an empty fuel tank, Chris and I found ourselves paddling over to the site in a motorless power boat. Grateful enough for its roominess once we got it there we began recording the paintings. We were rewarded with a strongly painted turtle and a peculiar group of animal forms, two of which portrayed only the heads and necks of unidentified creatures. There are rumours of another site on Sandford Lake nearby, and north of White Otter, near Patricia Lake, the Camp Owakonze boys have located a small one. Eastward again a further report comes from Upper Scotch Lake.

130

Site #223
White Otter
Lake

Frances Lake paintings, Site #208

Hansen Lake setting, Site #215

From McInnes' notes

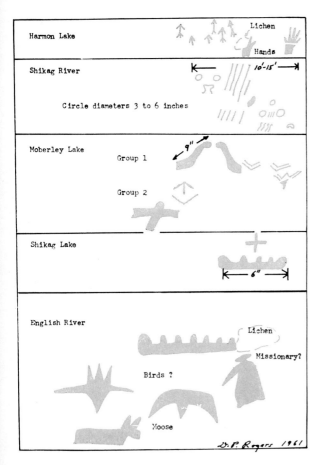

Without Rogers' drawings, which are reproduced here, our sampling of this area would be inadequate. Understandably he has not attempted to show nuances of strength or faintness in the pigment, but he has recorded the major lichen encroachments. The English River site he illustrates is on the upper river near its sources, just north of Selwyn Lake. The Shikag sites lie north of this again, the Moberley Lake one to the east. Moberley empties into the Brightsands River, along which yet another site has recently been reported. Farther north the river flows into Harmon Lake. Here is the only site in the area I have so far recorded, flying in from Port Arthur with Jack Snider in 1963.

Von Rosen's sites on Barrel and Ken lakes should be well worth visiting. On the former he found a handprint, two human figures (one horned), a wolf-like animal, and an obscure one that could be either bison or moose. The Ken Lake setting is a sheer 150-foot cliff along the base of which are painted arrows, handprints, tally marks, one large animal, and either a sun or a very abstract turtle.

132

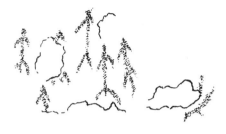

Harmon Lake, Site #151

Site #152,
Kitchiwatchi
Lake

flaking
here
shows clear
evidence
that some
of this face
has been
hammered
off

At Harmon, as at Abamatagwia, we have an assortment of sauromorphs, but these more closely resemble human forms. The rock here varies from a coarse pegmatite to a micaceous gneiss, and many of the original paintings are badly weathered.

Northward again, and east of Sioux Lookout, although I have an adequate sampling, there may remain as many as a dozen unrecorded sites, including four so far reported: on Sturgeon Lake opposite Hudson's Bay Point, on Barnard Lake, and more vaguely located on Savant and Brennan lakes. This disposes of all the west-central hinterland except for the easternmost portion approaching Lake Nipigon, and here again there are sites still to be recorded. On the Harmon Lake trip we stopped off at Gull Bay Indian Reserve to check with local trappers. When everyone

had had his say, adding nothing to what I had already learned there three years earlier, an old man who had remained modestly in the background came up, borrowed my pen and made a neat mark on the shore of Kitchiwatchi Lake. We landed there on our way back to be rewarded by the neat little painting of a Maymaygwayshi, with typical split head, which is illustrated here. The flaking that has removed most of the weird animal near it, I regret to say was clearly hammered off by a thoughtless souvenir hunter.

Sites on Obonga and Ottertooth lakes still elude us. In the summer of '66 Keith Denis organized a weekend expedition to investigate them, only to be turned back by a cloudburst that dropped three inches of rain in as many hours to wash out the Armstrong road for nearly a week. It

Lac des Iles,
Site #249

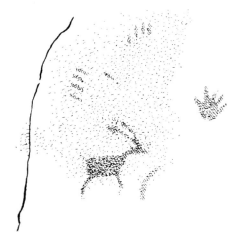

to a depth of a foot and a half, and roughly outlined by a six-inch high ridge of excavated earth. This, studied and recorded by Kenneth Dawson in 1962, has no counterpart I know of in the Shield country, but offers an interesting comparison with a number of effigies outlined in stone boulders in the Whiteshell district of southeast Manitoba, recorded by Richard Sutton of the Manitoba Museum. Recently Dawson has been doing an exciting dig on an island on Whitefish Lake, roughly thirty miles southwest of Fort William, to establish that the area had supported a much larger prehistoric population than had formerly been supposed.

At the east end of Whitefish Lake is a 200-foot escarpment extending halfway around a small plateau where local rumours had placed a group of petroglyphs. My hope ran high when I located a barber who claimed to have seen numerous carvings of deer and other animals while hunting on the plateau some thirty years previously. But after three attempts to find them I was ready to concede defeat. Then Jack Snider wrote to say he had located some carvings by a bush road south of the plateau, and that summer, guided by Irene Dawson, Peter and I recorded them. They were in no way similar to the barber's description, and a crudely scratched Union Jack, among other details, indicated a very recent origin.

The paintings on Pictured Lake, not far from Whitefish, have already been described (p. 75). In '66, having never been satisfied with my photographs, I persuaded Jack Snider

was Keith who finally located a man who could pin-point a site on Lac des Iles, over which I had flown once without spotting a single likely-looking rock. It turned out, when I finally recorded the site, that the rock was as effectively hidden as the second site at Darky Lake. Faint handprints and a deer-like animal were on the main face; but the figure on the left, again in the split head style, was in itself an ample recompense for the long search. Farther west, on a long irregular lake called Mooseland, is another possible site.

Between Lac des Iles and the Lakehead is Dog Lake, a source of the Kaministikwia River. On the portage from Little Dog there is a ground effigy of a dog scooped out of the soil

134

to come along with his camera, without an inkling of the shock I was in for. The magnificent canoe (reproduced on the title page) was just as I remembered it. But on the other face I stared in consternation at a dozen paintings *I had never seen before!*

I have only two excuses: my inexperience then, and the nature of this rock face, a curving, smoothly sculptured granite surface that sunlight threw into such strong relief that the faint paintings on a dark background simply vanished. But they became quite clear as the sun disappeared under heavy clouds and before the rain came I was able to make a careful sketch of the most distinct and interesting one, which is reproduced here.

The Nipigon Country

As early as 1958 I had found, in Harlan Smith's brief *Album of Pre-historic Canadian Art,* reproductions of drawings made by McInnes of paintings on a Cliff Lake in Kenora District. The only Cliff Lake I knew of was just off the Red Lake road, and my bafflement when I compared paintings I found there with McInnes' has already been described. It was not until I went through the geologist's field notes in Ottawa (through the courtesy of the Geological Survey of Canada) that I found the simple answer. There was another Cliff Lake, on the Mud River, north of Lake Nipigon, and this was his reference. In 1965, Chris and I drove up to Armstrong, and got a lift in to Cliff Lake on a tower-servicing flight that

allowed us three hours between drop-off and pick-up. Since McInnes had recorded only half a dozen paintings this seemed to be a reasonable time allowance.

But even as we circled for a landing I sensed that I had miscalculated. Here was a mere sliver of water eight miles long flanked on either side by one sheer cliff after another. The highest and most extensive one invited us to land beside it. Minutes later in the silence that followed the disappearing roar of the pilot's take-off we were paddling towards a dark wall of rock that loomed high on the east shore.

Almost at once I recognized one of the two animals in McInnes' drawings. But thereafter we paddled past

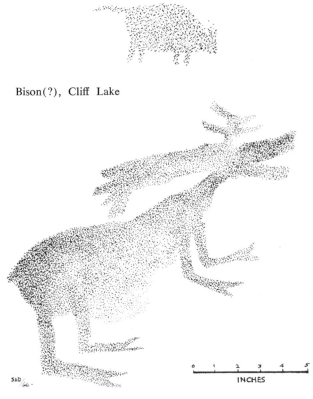

Bison(?), Cliff Lake

Pictured Lake
(*see* page 75)

INCHES

Cliff Lake, Site #119   *Photograph by Peter Dewdney*

rock after rock that had either been smeared or had accumulated the colour of vanished forms for centuries. The latter impression was reinforced by the occasional suggestion of the edge of such a form, sometimes against a patch of red, sometimes, and equally hard to see, against the dark basaltic rock. We fell to work feverishly at tracing and photographing the more discernible ones. In an hour we had run out of tracing paper. An hour later we had used up most of our film, but saved

our last exposures in case the promise of another site on the west side was fulfilled. It was. And just as we heard the first distant hum of our approaching aircraft we were looking over a third site we had found on re-crossing to the east side. And so, as Cliff Lake sank into the misty horizon behind us, I found myself repeating a famous phrase "I will return!"

The following year, with Ken and Irene Dawson's son Dane as an assistant, I did return. It had puzzled me to have found only one of McInnes'

136

drawings on the previous visit, but the answer was clear when we landed at the foot of a big cliff—one of the few outcrops of granite on the lake. Here were McInnes' feathered human figure, thunderbird, and canoes. But apparently he had ignored, as he had left out similarly enigmatic material on other sites, the peculiar abstractions illustrated here. Nowhere had I seen such contrasting styles within a small group, their separate origins emphasized by the distinct variations of pigment. The dreamlike "legs-that-walk-by-themselves" and associated symbols in a bright orange ochre emphatically differed from the "lone Indian" in a dull ochre so impure that it could only be described as a dirty brown; and whereas the former was painted with coarse, finger-width lines, the latter showed detail, as in the fingers of one hand, so fine that at first they escaped my notice. The "double-cross" painted over the canoe also differed in colour, and the canoe was painted in a fourth hue of the ochre basic to all. This overlapping and the obscuring lime deposit over the human figure both offered evidence of considerable age, although here there was none of the patination (or smearing) so typical of the main site farther down the lake. Yet weathering had taken its toll, too, on other paintings nearby, particularly the figure barely recognizable as human with its unusual centre line. The three "horse-shoes" by contrast seemed strong and presumably recent.

Dane and I had come prepared to stay overnight, but unprepared for the procession of thunderstorms that passed overhead until the first grey of dawn, with lightning so continuous that we could almost have worked by it. We rose early and got back to the rock, not knowing how many more paintings we would encounter before our pick-up in the afternoon. As it turned out we found two more sites that day, to bring the total up to six in a concentration of petrographs that is only exceeded by the Hickson-Maribelli sites north of the Churchill River in Saskatchewan, and by the Bon Echo sites on Lake Mazinaw in southeast Ontario.

By far the largest number of paintings was along the thousand feet of rock wall which, we learned, Chris and I had not thoroughly covered the year before. There were three main groups, designated III, IV, and VIII,

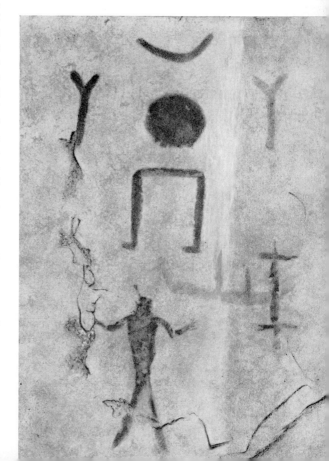

Site #262,
Cliff Lake,
Face III

Face III,
Site #219

the first and last on a dark trap-like rock which made the fainter details so difficult to distinguish even with the naked eye that tracings were impossible, sketching tedious and confusing, and even the colour photographs —as I was to learn when I had them developed—inadequate. Both III and VIII were smoothed by glaciation, but the former face seemed to have been grooved *vertically* by glacial action, which I still regard as impossible. With so little contrast we came back to work on it after the sun came out, only to find (as a few days later at Pictured Lake) that it threw the glacial grooving into relief and made the paintings almost invisible. Only

138

Site #219,
Face IV

McInnes' animal stands out on Face III; the vertical pattern that shows in the reproduction is due to streaking from lime deposits.

The left portion of Face IV illustrated here is on granitic rock, with some paintings so badly weathered that I have not attempted to include them. Face VIII was the most frustrating one on the lake to record, and of the confusion to the left I can only say that I erred on the side of clarity! None of the figures that *can* be distinguished vary from the regional style: there are abstracted human figures, the usual canoes, and some

Site #219,
Face IV continued

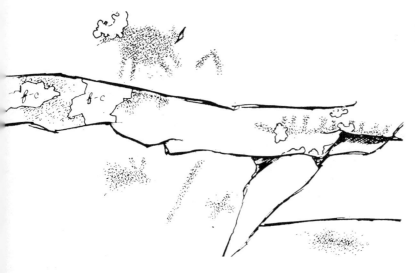

vague abstractions of which two or three might originally have represented animals. The animal reproduced from Face VIII is much fainter in the original. If, as I think, the long tail and great hump indicate a bison, a locale that is a week's canoe journey to the nearest grass country is an extraordinary place to find one.

Little more than the lichen-obscured sauromorph and vague animal shown on this page appear on the other east shore site. On the opposite side of the lake the second site, counting from the south end, is also small, displaying only the figure illustrated and a few vague abstractions. The third site offers little more. The one strong painting begins with a fairly definite head, but trails off into a vagueness that fails even to achieve

the distinction of being called an enigma! And the one small but pleasing design above it to the left is partly obscured by lichen. The fourth site is more extensive, with four groups of paintings, on the last of which are the charming little drawings of an animal —likely, at this latitude, a woodland caribou—and a man. The man is very like two figures I found in Saskatchewan, both of which had a similar projection from the head that I took for a pipe. Here the alternative might be a bird's bill, though I regard this as unlikely. All else on this site is abstract and vestigial, except for the tally marks, canoe, and stick figure reproduced from Face I.

Indeed, the overriding impression of the Cliff Lake setting is one of an age-hallowed place, where paintings

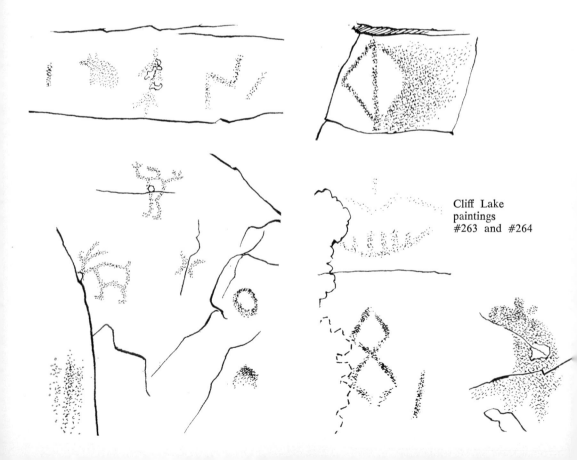

Cliff Lake
paintings
#263 and #264

were made at intervals over long periods of time. More than half of them are indecipherable and many more nearly so. But we cannot blame this on the possibility of a more easily weathered rock, for the glaciated sections have remained almost intact since the Ice Age. Perhaps the paint does not bond so well on basic rocks as compared with the acidic granite. Otherwise most of the paintings must be very old.

The previous summer Chris and I had gone on a wild goose chase to a small lake east of Inspiration Lake, a short flight from Armstrong, where the rock rose 80 feet above another 100 of rockfall. But as I flew over Inspiration on the way back from Cliff Lake I saw a number of impressive sheer faces that led me to wonder

whether my informant's "east of Inspiration" shouldn't have read "on the east side of Inspiration." On the other side of Lake Nipigon I suspect that another site or two will come to light, although I made two unrewarding boat trips into Humboldt Bay, and flew over Ombabika Bay, where the rumours of rock paintings seem to have had their source.

Just east of the south end of Lake Nipigon it took me two attempts to find a site on Barbara Lake. With John Chambers, a fellow artist from London, I turned off Highway 11 into a maze of lumber roads out of which we emerged on the shore of the wrong lake. Finally finding Barbara, we explored some fifteen miles of shoreline quite fruitlessly. Two years later, having finally found someone who could

Site #264,
Cliff Lake,
Face I

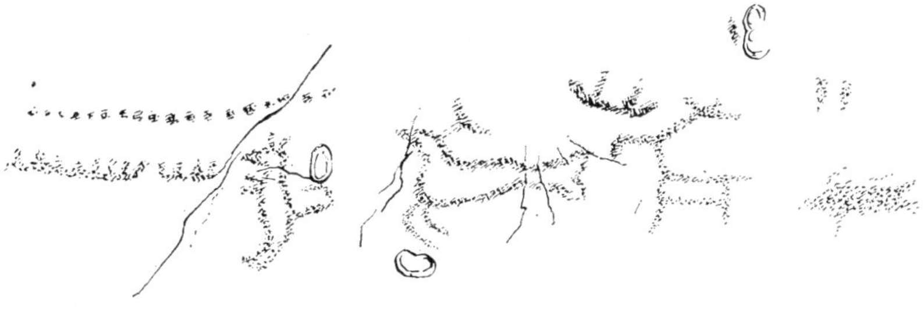

Barbara Lake,
Site #193,
Face IV

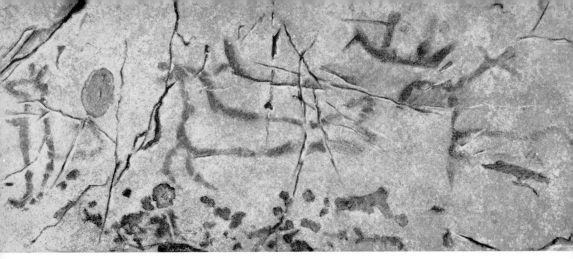

Barbara Lake, Site #193, Face IV in part

pin-point the site, I flew in from Geraldton and recorded it, only to discover that John and I had missed it by less than a quarter of a mile.

It was a natural miss. Like the Cache Bay site the Barbara Lake one is tucked away in a small blind bay whose entrance is so well screened that one could paddle past it a dozen times without noticing the channel. The paintings are scattered along the base of a coarse granite formation, partly smoothed by glacial action and kept free of lichens by periodic flooding. All are small, some tiny, as in the case of the hand, obviously not a print. The viewer can readily pick out four canoes and recognize two other likely ones under a row of tally marks. The central animal in the right-hand group is clearly a composite—half fish and half quadruped. This and the squirrel-like figure are both unique.

But my chief interest centred on the pair of animals facing each other, the one on the left apparently intended to be a reversal of the one on the right. The latter so strongly reminded me of the lion passant on the British coat of arms that it called to mind having read somewhere—I have yet to rediscover the reference—of a solution to the dilemma that arose when a totemless Anglo-Saxon married an Ojibwa woman. If the father had no totem the children would have none to inherit and how then would they know whom *not* to marry? For to marry someone of your own totem, even though there was no blood relationship whatever, was a sort of incest. But there was an easy solution: the British lion! I am inclined to believe the story if only because the word "lion" is the almost invariable translation advanced by Ojibwa interpreters for Mishipishiw. But although I have met a Loon, two Sturgeons and several Bears, I have yet to encounter an Ojibwa Lion!

142

Northeast Superior Shore

Ever since finding Schoolcraft's Agawa paintings on the Lake Superior shore I have been trying to locate his south shore site with such negative results that I am inclined to think they were painted on a softer rock from which they weathered into oblivion. At the beginning of my search for the north shore site I had focussed on "Les Petits Ecrits," a little cove near Schreiber marked on maps to this day. Then Keith Denis dug up a number of historical references to pictures along the northeast shore, including those of Agassiz, Bigsby, and Delafield. The last-named described one site as "the picture gallery of Lake Superior," but made it clear that the pictures were made by scraping the coarse dark leafy lichen known as rock tripe from a ruddy-hued rock. Nevertheless, after finding a major group of rock paintings at Agawa, I was sure that there would be more, and a vague report from a commercial fisherman at Mamainse, who thought he had seen some paintings up near Michipicoten, was all the encouragement I needed.

As soon as Highway 17 was completed between Montreal River and Marathon I was on it, stopping off wherever it touched a lake settlement to inquire of old-timers about the presence of the paintings I sought. But whether it was Batchewana, Michipicoten Harbour, Heron Bay, or Schreiber the story was the same: "Sure I heard there were some, but that was a long time ago." One set of rumours centred around the rough shore just north of Agawa, and names

Barbara Lake, Face II

like Gargantua, Devil's Warehouse, and the like encouraged me to hope that this was a good place to look. Access was not easy. Few local people ventured along the shore except tourist operators and commercial fishermen who had decked-in power boats, and the number of fishermen was dwindling with the depredations made by the lamprey on their annual catch. Even fishing and hunting for sport lured only a few along a shore where fog and high winds offered alternate hazards; havens were few and far between.

In the summer of '61 I took two weeks off from work on the first edition of this book to holiday with my wife and Chris at Agawa Beach. Keith Denis and his family were camped there, as well as Carl Atwood—entomologist, and a member of Quetico's Scientific Advisory Committee—with his wife and a daughter. Word came that Bill Collins, a veteran fisherman and guide at Mamainse, knew of paintings in Mica Bay, and on a late afternoon he guided us to the spot: a small but rugged granite headland. Sure enough there were paintings, on a rock face 20 feet above the water. Like the Killarney paintings they seemed to have been painted in an oil medium, laid on so thick that brush marks were still

visible in a few places. More curiously the colour was mostly yellow ochre, with white pigment mixed into some brush strokes and black into others. Crude and acculturated, they could neither be accepted as authentically aboriginal nor dismissed as coming from a frivolous hand. It was rather as if they had been the work of a canoe-man of mixed origins from a passing fur brigade, forced to lay over till a storm blew itself out, who had painted it as a simple gesture to half-remembered deities for luck on his current voyage.

Carl and Keith had already lined up a trip in Bill Collins' 32-foot gasoline launch to explore the mysteries of the Devil's Frying Pan and other intriguing features of the shore north of Agawa. With a large wheelhouse, cabins fore and amidships, and a small deck aft there was lots of room; so all the males from the three camps went along including me and Chris, leaving the womenfolk to socialize in our absence. Towing a row-boat, we set out on a smooth, sunny day, passed Mica Bay and Montreal Island and Agawa without incident, and headed north for the Devil's Warehouse and Frying Pan. The latter was a wicked-looking reef, seething dramatically even in that mild swell, but the "warehouse" turned out to be

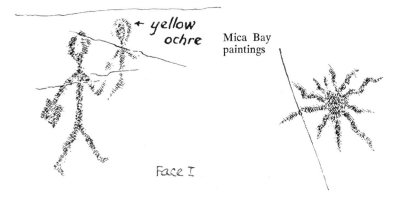

← yellow ochre

Mica Bay paintings

Face I

a shallow, wide-mouthed cave, its sole feature a pile of rock fragments that had obviously fallen from the ceiling. We explored some nearby cliffs, but the rock was an altered sediment of a highly friable sort overgrown everywhere with lichens. By early evening we had passed Gargantua and entered Indian Harbour where we dropped anchor for the night. Exploring the shore in the rowboat after supper we found lots of rock faces, but no paintings.

Returning southward, we called in for a look at Gargantua Harbour, once a favourite rendezvous for cruising yachtsmen and their families, with a huge rotting dock that had trembled on occasion under the dancing feet of dozens of couples from a score of yachts in the snug little harbour. Now the yachts are rare and such celebrations are seen no more. We walked across the point to a headland where the rising wind blew fresh in our faces from across the chilly waters of the world's greatest fresh water sea; and found a place where generations of waterborne travellers had left their initials or the name of their boat painted or pecked in the rock. There were promising rock faces along the shore with ledges where an aboriginal artist might stand and paint. I wandered off to look at them. Groping through some heavy bush cover for access down to such a ledge I suddenly found myself stepping on nothing and a split second later dangling by one hand from an instinctively grasped spruce bough. Then the branch broke and I found myself on the ledge—a mere two inches under my dangling foot! But neither then nor later that morning did I find any paintings.

The trip back to Mamainse was a nightmare. Racing along with great waves full abeam, the spray whipped from the white-caps as they formed, one moment in a trough looking up at a looming wave crest, then rising, rising at a sickening list to its peak, where we had a brief glimpse of a wild sea and spume shooting high on the rocks a mere half-mile to leeward, before dropping away on our other beam-end into the following trough! Over and over again. That was tolerable, but there was real suspense when the engine stopped and Bill disappeared into the bowels of the boat while we drifted out of control, the ugly shore a little closer each time we glimpsed it from a wave crest. Then Bill came up grinning. The gasoline filter had gummed up, he had cleaned it out, and a minute later we were on our way. He repeated the performance as we paused later in the lee of Montreal Island opposite Agawa beach, where—we were to learn—our wives were even then contemplating widowhood as they stood on the shore and watched the huge breakers thundering in. For a final touch, we sought the entrance between the wicked reefs that guarded the entrance to Mamainse Harbour. Bill headed full speed towards a white cauldron of foam in what seemed a deliberate attempt at suicide, then swung sharply to port through a narrow turbulent channel and into calm water.

Year after year thereafter, I made my enquiries along the newly built highway with no result, until it became clear that we could only answer the question by a first-hand search. It was George MacGillivray, publisher of the Fort William *Times-Journal*, and descendant of the great Nor'-Wester of the same name, who made the donation that sparked a Lakehead Historical Society expedition along the northeast Superior shore. Ken Dawson, Keith Denis, and I, with Jack Snider as photographer and scribe, headed east out of Port Arthur on a Friday evening in the Society's truck for a long drive into the night, on which we narrowly missed running down the lagging twin of a calf moose that had crossed the beam of our headlights. Arriving finally at the mouth of the Pic River we found our diesel launch and spread our bedrolls on the hard benches in the cabin to await the dawn. With its first light pilot Bob McCuaig and crew of one turned up, and we were on our way.

Les Ecrits, Lake Superior

Our object: to find and record rock paintings and to locate the site of Delafield's "picture gallery," to interview old-time residents about early times, and to do some archaeological reconnaissance and sampling at likely points along the shore. No four men began a trip more optimistically; few deserved so little luck.

It was difficult—so perfect was the weather as we traversed the loneliest stretch of the old fur route between Montreal and the northwest—to see the shore for what it was: a bleak, inhospitable coastline, subject to unpredictable shifts of wind that offered the alternatives of fog or high seas, miles and miles of which—with the great lake reaching out westward toward infinity—invited neither hunter, fisherman, nor home-seeker to linger long. Nor, in my belief, has it ever attracted even a small indigenous population. And yet, what men for what reason made the pits in the coarse pebble and boulder beaches along that shore, named, after the first that were studied by Emerson and his crew, the Puckasaw pits? We found a few that had not been known before down near Otterhead (named after a rock that looks like an otter), but could make no sense out of them. Even as ritual nests for aboriginal dream fasts they were bunched together too often and varied too much in their proportions.

Wherever we stopped Dawson dug, Denis queried any inhabitant he could locate, and Dewdney scanned the rocks. But none of us found the rewards we had hoped for. At Puckasaw we gloomily stared at the grave of a twentieth-century man who had come to stay, and at the ghosts among the young trees of the little lumber city that had been a hustling community of fifteen hundred souls when I was no longer a boy. We docked for the night at a summer cottager's camp (one of only two we saw on the whole trip) in Otter Bay; went as much farther south as our time allowed, then turned back. I still had some hope. We had by-passed Oiseau Bay on the way down, as well as the promisingly named Picture Rock Harbour. But Oiseau Bay contained nothing, and my usual optimism was nearly gone as we neared the mouth of White River, a favourite stop-over for the voyageurs, well sheltered from the wind by the ramparts of granite behind which the river emptied.

As we approached we re-read Major Delafield's words of 1843: "This place is composed of granite cliffs presenting perpendicular faces to the lake. Upon these walls are figured images of deer, moose, canoes, Indians with bows, all pretty well delineated, some by Indians and some by voyageurs. The base of the rock is red feldspar, so that when the rust and lichens which now cover them are rubbed off by stone or iron, a bright red surface is produced which forms the images. This is a common stopping place for canoes bound either up or down the lake, when high winds prevent their progress, and this is no doubt the cause of its having become the picture gallery of Lake Superior."

I was not long in getting ashore and climbing the ascending blocks to search their faces for whatever lingering trace of lichen glyphs there might be—though I knew this was unlikely —and for the paintings I hoped might also have been made. There were no paintings and no glyphs. What puzzled all of us was that there was so little rock tripe that there were few places where such designs could be scraped today. There could be no doubt about the location, even though Delafield had confusedly called it "the Petit des Escrit." The extensive galleries of rock, their fracture planes an undeniable red, distinguished the place from any other along that shore, and we all agreed that this was the site of Les Ecrits.

There was one last hope of finding some paintings—in Picture Rock Harbour, or as some maps called it, Picture Cove. We took our kicker into the bay and headed toward a most promising rock at the northeast end. As I viewed the great overhang from closer and closer I was sure that my luck had turned.

But it hadn't.

Darkness was falling as the expedition dropped me off at Pays Platt for a rendezvous with Bert McGooey. First thing in the morning, with Bert at the wheel of a fast Lands and Forests outboard, we were off for the little cove called Les Petits Ecrit. It was another perfect day, but it was rough enough when we emerged from the shelter of a series of offshore islands that we were happy to round an ugly headland into the small haven, land on the pebble beach, and head for the nearby rocks.

The famous glacial geologist, Louis

147

Agassiz, had stopped here more than a century ago, and had described "various animals, canoes full of men, &c., together with various fabulous monsters, such as snakes with wings, and the like, cut out of the lichens." He had also noted that "these pictures were of various dates, as was shown by the various degrees of distinctness, as the rock was either laid quite bare, or the black lichens had more or less completely recovered possession of it."

Petits made sense, for the rock formation here, identical with that at Les Ecrits, was in less than a tenth of the scale. On the rocks I found barely enough surviving lichen to scrape out an experimental thunderbird. From the water this showed up as a faint, dull colour—scarcely Delafield's "bright, red surface." And why so little lichen now, where there was once so heavy a growth? Lichenologists tell me that changes in the atmosphere can affect lichen growth; and it may be that the occasional presence of sulphide fumes from the paper mills at Terrace Bay and Marathon have discouraged lichen growth at both sites.

In 1966, on my way west, I stopped as usual to take another look at the Agawa paintings. It was late evening when I passed the scenic lookout point on Highway 17, a couple of miles past the Agawa camping grounds, and turned left on the gravel road to the picnic grounds and parking lot from which a pathway leads down to the site of the paintings. That night, sleeping in my Volkswagen bus, I was awakened again and again by thunder and the heavy drumming of rain on my roof. After a hasty breakfast I followed the trail down to the site. The great lake was calm, but the access ledge—so frequently under the lash of its waves—was wet on this occasion from the night's rain, and water was still dripping from the rain-soaked overburden at the top of the cliff. It was my first chance here to observe how a heavy rainfall affected the rock faces where the paintings were. All of them had escaped direct rainfall and dripping, but with seepage it was a different story; Face I was soaked, while the other rock faces were bone dry. The explanation was simple. The whole cliff leaned out over the water at a sufficient angle that dripping from above fell clear, and one could see that only a driving rain would wet the whole surface. The seepage, however, which dripped clear from a wide overhang 20 feet above the other paintings, continued its downward course uninterrupted to wet the whole of Face I. A slight lime content in this moisture had discouraged lichen growth, but had added a slight film to the paintings; and the frequent wet-

Les Petits Ecrits,
Lake Superior

ness had accelerated weathering here to the point that, had I been unaware of the cause, I would never have suspected the four canoes painted here to have been of the same age as the other Myeengun paintings.

I was disturbed to discover that work on the catwalk begun the year before to reduce the hazards of viewing the petrographs had been suspended. Not only that, but the last flight of wooden stairs had disappeared. Obviously the winter ice had been at work. Later that morning I learned from the Park staff how formidable the problem of providing public access to the place had proved. Over the last few years the lake has remained open all winter, and winter gales pile the ice up to a height of 30 feet. Small wonder that the steel supports, set deep in the solid granite, have been twisted and bent, and the lower stairs torn away. Lands and Forests' officials are studying the problem, but it may be that future viewers who prefer not to venture out on the rock ledge from which the paintings were made will have to be satisfied with a boat trip around the point from Sinclair Cove where the Department of Transport has recently completed a public dock. Even then, whenever the wind is westerly, they will not be able to get closer than 20 feet to the rocks, so will miss the smaller and fainter paintings.

I am no longer as sure as I was about identifying all of the Schoolcraft reproductions of Myeengun's paintings. In fact, I am now quite certain that the faint abstraction to the right of the horse, even if Ching-

wauk was right in reproducing it as a turtle, was *not* painted by Myeengun or any of his men. It differs too radically in style and technique and is weathered almost to disappearance in an area that gets the same protection as those around it.

Incidentally, in scanning Ojibwa birchbark scrolls of the Midaywiwin for material that might relate to the rock paintings, I have run across occasional representations of Mishipizhiw. On two of these the "Big Lynx" is clearly recognizable as a panther. In every other instance the horns of supernatural power are present, while other features vary. Of five paintings by Norval Morrisseau four have horns *plus* a dragon-like tail, and one has the stubby tail of a lynx. The larger of the two renderings of the water deity at Agawa is the only one I know of that shows the cheek whiskers of the lynx.

149

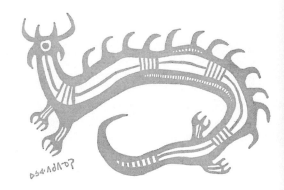

From drawing
by Norval Morriseau

Northeastern Hinterland

Northwest of Michipicoten the Hudson Bay Lowlands come within fifty miles of the Lake Superior shore, and the width of the Shield region between Long Lac and Lake Missinaibi narrows to an average of eighty miles. Consequently, the watersheds of all the great northern rivers that drain into James Bay—the Attiwapiskat, Albany, and various branches of the Moose, after a longer or shorter tortuous passage through the Shield—enter the flat Hudson Bay plain, rockless except where they cut through bedding planes of limestone. A drunken informant at Matachewan told me that there were paintings near the confluence of the Abitibi River and the Moose, and I have heard rumours of a site on the Winisk River. Unfortunately, the old men who travelled these rivers early in the century are dying off one by one. But I am still hopeful that I will hear of a modest site or two on a low limestone face in the Hudson Bay lowlands.

There is one exception to this general flatness that I was able to reach while flying with Rod Standfield on the eastern phase of his polar bear count. On the same day that I saw twelve of the great-pawed beasts from 500 feet—overhead—we turned south along the James Bay coast from Cape Henrietta Maria, then inland to a remarkable plateau called Sutton Ridge. Here nestle two small lakes, with great ramparts lining the narrows between, in places rising sheer from the water. But the rock was very rough, and when we landed for a brief chat with the Cree proprietor of what is probably the most isolated fly-in camp in Ontario, at Hawley Lake, we were assured that he had never seen or heard of rock paintings in the area.

To come back to the narrow "isthmus" of the Shield formation northeast of Lake Superior, only two sites have turned up between Long Lac and Lake Missinaibi, neither yet recorded. One on Manitowik is not

150

Horwood Lake
in winter
(note summer level
shown by ice above)

likely to be seen again, having been flooded out some thirty years ago by a lumber dam. The other has been pin-pointed on Mackay Lake, a short hop east of Long Lac.

Fifty miles north of the Missinaibi sites is Brunswick Lake. A flight from Kapuskasing in '65 yielded nothing but some bright red iron stains in the southeast corner of the lake. But the only report I have is self-contradictory, possibly out of the kind of confusion that I have run into before, when an informant identified an un-named lake with the nearest named one.

Sixty miles east of Missinaibi is Horwood Lake where two sites were found by the widely ranging MacFie several years ago. In the warm months both are under 20 feet of water; only in the early spring, when the stop-logs have been taken out of the dam, does the lake return to its former level. So in April of '63 I found myself flying in from Gogama on a ski-shod Beaver for the novel experience of recording a site from the ice. None of the paintings is strong, but I doubt if their faintness is due to the annual flooding, for others I have seen, subject to seasonal flooding over much longer periods, vary widely in strength. As the drawings here illustrate, nearly all the forms are abstract excepting the possible thunderbird.

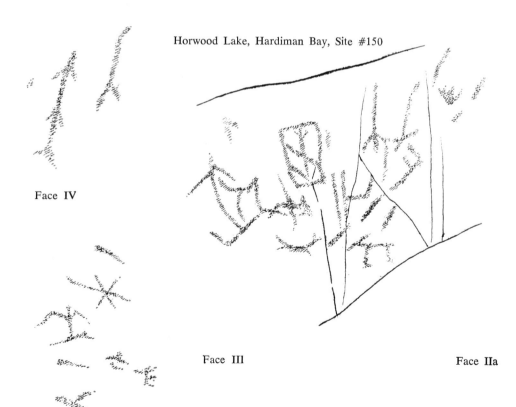

Horwood Lake, Hardiman Bay, Site #150

Face IV

Face III

Face IIa

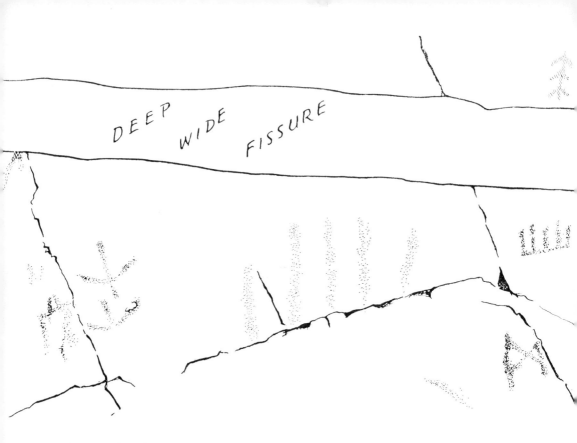

DEEP WIDE FISSURE

Matachewan Lake, Site #244

The northeasternmost site recorded so far in Ontario is close to the upper bend of the Montreal River that flows (to distinguish it from several other rivers so named in Canada) into Lake Timiskaming. Access is by water and one portage from the village of Matachewan, an hour's drive west of Swastika. If the two figures shown here are bird tracks, they are the sole example I know of in the Shield. The faint vertical abstraction with chevrons may represent a tree.

Much farther north, beyond Cochrane and on the northern edge of the Shield, a likely petroglyph site continues to elude me, although I was sent a sketch of the figures—mostly abstract—and another of the route to the site. Unfortunately the original source goes back thirty years and the area is riddled with lumber roads; nor could I find anyone who knew of a rock outcrop on the river anywhere near the place marked on the sketch.

152

Gogama remains a promising centre for pictograph-hunting, with three sets of paintings reliably reported in the vicinity; one on Devil's (or Wizard) Lake, one on Rush Lake, and a third on Beaver Lake. In the Timagami area Dr. Tom Lovegrove has traced and photographed two small sites he discovered on the lake itself. One features a snake-like form, the other consists of crosses and tally marks. Neither, apparently, was known to the George Turner who took me to the two other even slighter sites on the same lake. On nearby Obabika Lake is another site not yet recorded.

It is puzzling that repeated visits to Sudbury failed to turn up paintings at nearby Matagamasi Lake, although I had picked up reports there of far less accessible ones as early as '59. It was George Stock, historian for Falconbridge Mines, who not only informed me of it but arranged to take me there. The illustrations omit the more vestigial paintings. My own interest centred on the human figure almost obliterated by seepage from a crack down the middle which has nourished a fine-grained black lichen. Obviously seepage must have begun *after* the painting had been made. Note, too, the wolf-like animal, painted with a naturalism that is rare in the Shield pictographs.

Face II, Site #150 (*see* page 150)

Matagamasi Lake,
Site #218, Face II

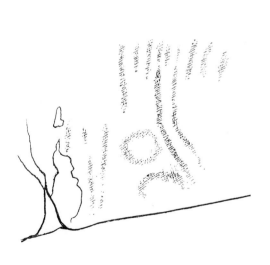

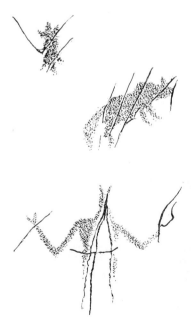

Former District Forester G. Coyne
examining flooded offerings,
Site #93

Photograph by Dean Conger,
National Geographic Society,
Whitefish Bay, Lake of the Woods

The fact that no new sites have
turned up along the old voyageur
route between the mouth of the
French River and the Ottawa River
has plagued me for five years. I have
finally traced the report of a huge
snake on the Georgian Bay shore
west of the French River to a group
of pictographs at the mouth of the
Serpent River. Informants on the
Reserve at Spragge told me that a
long time ago a group of huge snakes
had been seen on a rock near the
river mouth "with their heads all
pointing down," and that pictures of
them had been made on the rock
after the event. But these have disappeared, which strongly suggests that
they were scraped out from the lichen.

Thanks again to George Stock I
have a description of pictographs on
the French River from the diary of
John Macdonnel, published in 1793.
"Some leagues below Derreaud's
Rapids [which he places "two leagues"
below Recollet Falls] is the figure
of a man standing over an animal
that lays under him, with a sun on
one side and the moon on the other
side of him each surrounded by a
large circle—a little farthur on, is
at least sixteen figures of different
animals standing promiscuously together on the face of a steep Rock.
Amongst them may be seen fish,
flesh, and Tortoise, all of them painted
with some kind of Red Paint. These
figures are made by scratching the
Rock weed [moss] off the Rocks with
the Point of a knife or some other
instrument, Two leagues from Lake

"Prayer sticks" on clothing,
found at Site #105,
south of Devil's Bay, Lake of the Woods

155

Huron there is the figure of an ox which gives its name to a fine long View of the river called Lad du Boeuf."

Note the contradiction here; in the one sentence "Red Paint," and in the next "made by scratching." Though I have questioned Lands and Forests personnel and sportsmen who know the river, none of them has seen any such figures; and I think we must assume that Macdonnel was confusing lichen glyphs at this site with paintings he may have seen elsewhere. The same mystery applies to pictures mentioned by William Hawkins in his report of a canal survey he made of the Petawawa River in 1837, "engraven" on a rock wall 200 yards long and 150 feet high. They too, have disappeared, and I am reasonably sure that all three were lichen glyphs that have long ago grown in.

Southeast Ontario

In Southern Ontario a line drawn from Honey Harbour in Georgian Bay to Kingston at the outlet of Lake Ontario, here and there touching the northern shores of the Kawartha Lakes, roughly indicates the southern edge of the Canadian Shield in the province. Only where it cuts across the St. Lawrence to form the Thousand Islands does it leave Ontario for a brief excursion into the State of New York. South of this line the rocks are all of sedimentary types—limestones and shales—exposed only along lake shores and river banks.

The great exception to this rule is the Niagara escarpment. Capped by a durable dolomitic limestone this formation snakes its way from below Niagara Falls through Hamilton to Collingwood. Similar formations follow the shoreline of the Bruce Peninsula to Tobermory and reappear as Manitoulin Island. On a family excursion in '59 we checked the report of pictographs in Mindemoya Cave on Manitoulin, but found no trace of carvings or paintings. Another report, of a site near Hamilton, has been in the Museum files for years and only recently have I got wind of an informant now knowing its whereabouts. A cliff of similar rocks is on the west shore of Fayette Peninsula in northern Michigan, and here I recorded two sites. The fascinating sample illustrated here, as well as the others I recorded, has a phallic emphasis that suggests the crossing of a cultural boundary. In fact, I was told by a local farmer that figures painted on a third site farther down the shore had been so blatantly male that the management of a girls' camp nearby had had them defaced!

In the whole of Ontario, however, the only aboriginal rock paintings so far found on limestone occur on the north shore of the St. Lawrence River inside the city limits of Brockville, and of these only a canoe, partially obscured by iron stains, is recognizable. Local myth has it that an Iroquois party with English (!) prisoners decided to lighten the canoe of them. In the process the canoe was swamped and all or most of its occupants drowned. Each year thereafter, well

Painting near cave
at Site #81,
Burnt Bluff, Michigan

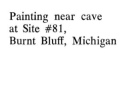

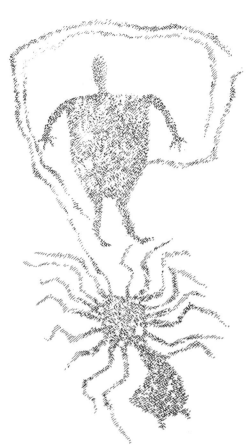

Site #191,
Brockville

into the 1800's, the survivors or their relatives returned to the place to renew the paintings. The Fulford family who owned the property, I was told, had "restored and enlarged" the paintings to the upper left. Now indecipherable, they give the appearance of having been coated with some substance which has since played host to disfiguring growths of algae or fungi.

It seems unlikely that any of the Iroquoian people, whose corn-raising practices determined their occupancy of relatively rockless country, put any pictographs on rock. And, though limestone is far less durable than granite, the fact that I have found paintings on limestone in the Rockies, and just south of the Shield edge in Saskatchewan and Manitoba suggests that if there had been any number of them in Southern Ontario at least a few should have survived.

157

Peterborough petroglyph
(surrounding rock
has been chalked
for photography)

Sole painting
in Brockville Narrows,
Site #192

To return to the Shield region of southeastern Ontario I know of only one site that is not yet recorded—on Rock Lake near the southern edge of Algonquin Park—and this consists only of a vague animal and a few tally marks. There is a petroglyph site on Sparrow Lake in the Muskoka District, and that is all. Mention has been made on earlier pages of the Mazinaw paintings and the glyphs near Nephton, north of Stony Lake. The only newly-recorded site is a mere wisp of a painting, shown here, to which I was guided by Herbert Sheridan of Brockville. It is situated at Brockville Narrows, just inside the Shield formation of the Thousand Islands, on a granite wall.

The unnatural blank in the Muskoka - Haliburton - Algonquin Park area, where there are plenty of suit-able settings for rock paintings, I have accounted for by the extensive lumbering operations in the late nineteenth century and early twentieth, when numerous lumber dams were built to float the logs out of the larger rivers. The new water levels have proved too useful to abandon so that when the original dams rot out they are usually replaced by more permanent structures. Only where the old levels are restored is it likely that any further rock paintings will be found.

This completes the roster of rock paintings in the Canadian Shield woodlands of Ontario as recorded to the end of 1966. The reader will now be ready to view them from the broader perspective of an anthropologist, and I pass my pen over to the initiator of our quest, Kenneth E. Kidd.

158

Anthropological Background

KENNETH E. KIDD

A NATION'S RESOURCES include many things. When one thinks of them, one is most likely to think first of all of agricultural, mineral, and forest resources, for these are primary; and then, secondly, of manufacturing and industrial potential. There is, however, besides these a multitude of assets which go to make up the total heritage, and among them one may well count anthropological and historical legacies. Part of the Canadian heritage is the complex of Indian rock paintings left by generations of woodland dwellers who inhabited the country before the white man arrived on its shores, and for some time thereafter.

It is indeed true that rock paintings are not limited to Ontario, to Canada, nor even to North America. The cave paintings of France and Spain and certain other parts of Europe have been known for many years, while those of Tassili in the Sahara desert have recently been discovered, studied, and admirably described by Henri Lhote. In Siberia, numerous sites have been found and described by the Russian archaeologist, Okladnikov. The South African rock paintings, many of them studied by the late Abbé Breuil, are justly famous, and each year adds fresh discoveries to their already large number. There is indeed no continent, and but few countries, which cannot claim to have some examples of this type of record from its past. In North America, the distribution of rock paintings is very great; in fact, few large areas which were suitable for making them were overlooked or neglected.

The first mention of these American paintings which has come to the present writer's attention appeared in the English periodical *Archaeologia* in 1781; generally speaking, they attracted little attention, however, either on the part of the antiquarians of the day, or of the many travellers who had the opportunity of seeing them. The first systematic attempt to record rock paintings on this continent was undertaken by Colonel Garrick Mallery in the United States. His eight-hundred–page report to the Secretary of the Smithsonian Institution, under the aegis of the Bureau of American Ethnology, and containing the results of his investigations from 1876 to 1893, forms the bulk of that Bureau's tenth annual report. Using the term "pictograph" as a generic designation to cover "picture-writing" in every sort of medium—bark, wood, bone, rock, copper, hide, and so on; whether painted, smeared, carved, scratched, pecked, or pounded—he made an invaluable record, extensively illustrated, of the examples of which he knew personally or by report.

Though Mallery concentrated upon sites within the borders of the United States, he included what he had learned about other sites in the Americas, and even beyond, but the only Canadian rock pictures actually illustrated in his report were carvings on the shores of Fairy Lake in Nova Scotia. As for other records of Canadian occurrences, a thorough search of the literature has not yet been made. But it is known that even before the turn of the century, some sites here and there across Canada had been noted; rock carvings and rock paintings had both been recorded in the far west before 1900. In Ontario, two men particularly were alert to and recorded graphically the occurrence of rock paintings. One of these, David Boyle, the first director of the Provincial Museum, recorded rock paintings at the large site at Bon Echo Lake, as well as those at two smaller sites north of Lake Timagami, on Diamond and Lady Evelyn Lakes. The other man, a geologist named McInnes, made sketches of such sites as he found while examining rock outcroppings on the shores of the Shield country lakes and rivers, during the course of work done in northwestern Ontario for the Geological Survey. Neither man was an artist, and each had to sketch under the exigencies of other work; yet despite some inaccuracies, their records are invaluable.

Drawing by David Boyle of detail on Face X (*see* page 96)

The idea from which the present survey stems had its beginnings in 1946, when Mr. A. E. Kundert, of Madison, Wisconsin, sent to the Royal Ontario Museum a small number of colour photo transparencies, showing rock paintings he had seen on Lake Mameigwess in the Lakehead area of Ontario. In one of them could be seen an animal which appeared to have a hump on its back, suggesting a bison. Bison in such heavily wooded, lake country would be an interesting phenomenon indeed and the matter aroused the writer's curiosity. This information was followed up by inquiries addressed to two well-known students of the history and lore of the Lakehead area to see what further evidence of rock paintings might be on record locally. Mr. Sigurd

161

Olson, the prominent naturalist, author, and conservationist, and Dr. Grace Lee Nute of the Minnesota Historical Society both replied that they knew of such occurrences at Hegman Lake, Minnesota. Professor Robert C. Dailey of the Department of Anthropology in the University of Toronto noted several occurrences during field work in Quetico Park.

The matter lay fallow for several years, and it was not until the Quetico Foundation enabled the writer to make a trip through Quetico Park for quite a different purpose that it was revived. On that trip, the writer was able to see for himself the splendid paintings of moose on the rocky ledges of Irving Island in Lac la Croix, which convinced him that they were worthy of recording. In 1957 the project got started. In that year, the Quetico Foundation kindly provided necessary funds to carry through the work for one summer, if a suitable recorder could be found and if the Royal Ontario Museum were agreeable to supervising it. This the Museum was happy to do, and chose Mr. Selwyn Dewdney to carry out the field work. He was an excellent choice, both because of his training in art and because of his experience in and knowledge of the woodland country where he would have to work. He had canoed extensively through it in his youth, knew and understood how to face its problems, and had a sympathetic attitude towards the native inhabitants. Thus the project was launched.

The Wilderness Research Center at Basswood Lake, Minnesota, was also interested in the project, and in each succeeding year has generously lent its support. The Ontario Department of Lands and Forests assisted in many ways, and it is safe to say that, without its help, much of the work could not

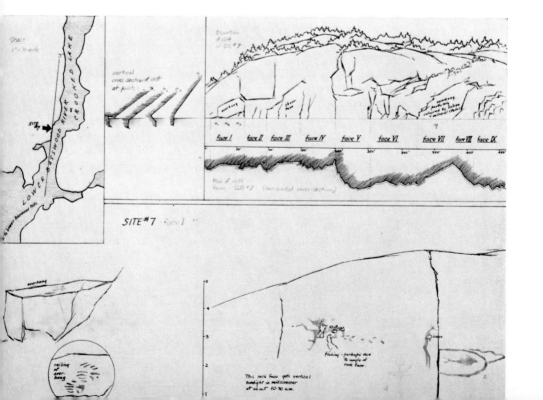

have been accomplished. Its personnel passed on information which came to them concerning the location of sites, and in numerous other ways its facilities aided in the recording programme. To all of these agencies, and to the many individuals who helped along the way, a debt of great gratitude is due, not only for direct aid, but also for encouragement and incidental support. Finally, the Royal Ontario Museum has happily been able to give increasing support to the recording project. It is the repository for the reproductions made by Mr. Dewdney, where students will have access to them for study, so far as is consistent with their good preservation.

Care has been taken to make the Museum's records as comprehensive and detailed as possible. Black and white line drawings to the scale of one inch to the foot show the disposition of all discernible paintings on each face of a given site, the elevation of the paintings above the water on the date of recording, the special features of the site (lichen growth, cracks, etc.), and the exact geographical location. Colour transparencies on file for the great majority of the sites record the landscape setting, relative variations in colour, and in many cases detailed close-ups (up to .5 metres) recording lichen growth, lime precipitates, flaking, and pigmentation. In addition Dewdney has executed full-size water colour copies of all the more significant and representative pictographs, many of which are reproduced in this book as half-tone photo-engravings. Finally, notes on the sites themselves, ethnological material related to the sites, and records of interviews with contemporary Indians are also on file, providing a wealth of supplemental data for future study. This information is available to responsible researchers.

It was possible to include only a part of this material in the present publication, but every effort has been made to cover it in as thorough and representative a way as the limits of space would allow. Actually there is at least a brief reference to every recorded site, and only a half dozen of the minor sites are left unrepresented in the illustrations.

The Canadian Shield country is a land of rocks, rivers, and lakes, with perhaps somewhat more water than land. The elevation is generally not great, although in some points it rises to as much as 4000 feet above sea level. Rapids and waterfalls are often impediments to navigation. The land is covered with a dense growth of mixed coniferous and deciduous forests, consisting of spruce, tamarack, jack pine, birch, and poplar. Except in the southernmost reaches, along the Rainy River drainage, and in the districts of Parry Sound, Muskoka, Nipissing, and southward, no hardwoods are present. The forest is inhabited by numerous species of animals, notably the beaver, otter, mink, fisher, foxes, wolves, black bears, and rabbits. Moose are now common, elk are absent, and caribou present only in small herds in parts of the area. Wildfowl are abundant in season, particularly ducks, geese, loons, and others which habitually continue northward for the breeding season. The streams and lakes abound in fish of many species. Snakes, though found occasionally, are not very abundant; they are the cause of much comment when seen.

163

Opposite:
a sample page from the Museum drawings, Crooked Lake site

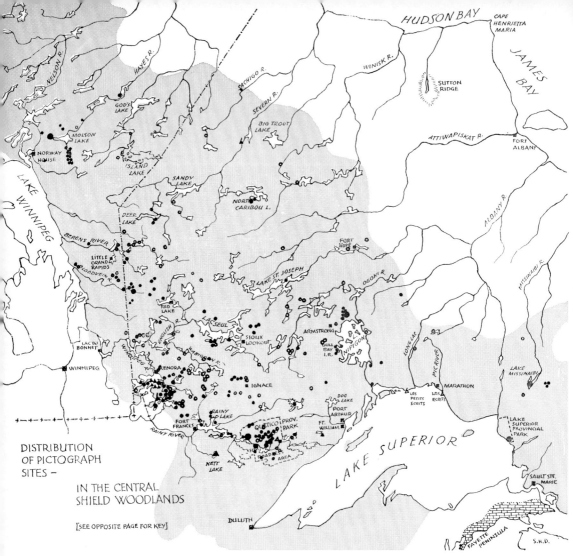

DISTRIBUTION
OF PICTOGRAPH
SITES –

IN THE CENTRAL
SHIELD WOODLANDS

[SEE OPPOSITE PAGE FOR KEY]

To its Indian inhabitants, the region must have been both a paradise and a severe challenge. Despite the dense forests, one could travel almost anywhere by water, using canoes in the summer and snowshoes and toboggans in the winter when the lakes and rivers were frozen. Food was usually reasonably abundant in the form of fish and game and berries, but at times it was hard to find, and hunger was the consequence for the unlucky hunter and his dependents. Materials for wigwams and tipis were everywhere, in the form of birch bark and poles, but they were impermanent. The skins of animals to be used as lodge coverings were harder to come by, but could usually be had for the effort; they were likewise sought for winter clothing. Winters were often bitterly cold and the snows deep; summers were hot, and accompanied by clouds of mosquitoes and other biting insects which made life miserable for all human inhabitants. Agriculture under aboriginal conditions was impracticable. Hunting and fishing were thus the only available means of subsistence in most areas (apart from a little berry-picking), and the former was subject to those cyclic variations in the game supply which periodically imposed severe hardships upon the inhabitants. In those parts of the Shield country where they could be had, the Indians were more fortunate in having the additional support of wild rice and maple sugar to help them through the lean months.

This land of shining waters and gloomy forest was the general environment in which the painters of the rock pictures were born, lived their lives, and went finally to their happy hunting ground. It was by turn benign and cruel, beautiful and harsh, ample and niggardly, but always inscrutable. To the Indian's mind, there must have been forces at work whose nature he could but dimly surmise, and it was therefore to him the part of wisdom to try to keep in their favour. Alternatively, some of these forces could be harnessed, so to speak, to cause injury or death to others, or by suitable rituals cajoled into assuming a friendly attitude to the supplicant. The world was to these people composed not only of the tangible and the visible but also of much which was invisible and immaterial.

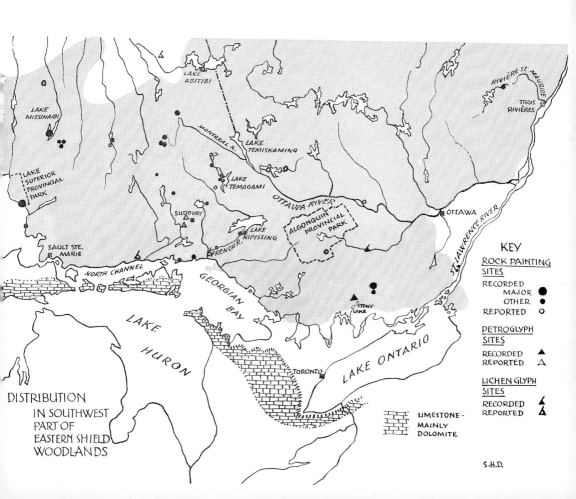

KEY

ROCK PAINTING SITES
RECORDED
MAJOR ●
OTHER ●
REPORTED ○

PETROGLYPH SITES
RECORDED ▲
REPORTED △

LICHEN GLYPH SITES
RECORDED ⚐
REPORTED ⚑

DISTRIBUTION IN SOUTHWEST PART OF EASTERN SHIELD WOODLANDS

LIMESTONE - MAINLY DOLOMITE

S.H.D.

The archaeological history of the country north of the Great Lakes is only beginning to be understood, but numerous students are interested in its pre-history. Mr. Thomas E. Lee, formerly of the National Museum of Canada, and Dr. Emerson F. Greenman, of the University of Michigan, have shown that there were human occupants at the edge of the ice sheets as they retreated northward some 8,000 to 9,000 years ago, and that later inhabitants made and used pottery. Long before pottery-making became known, however, there was a group, at least along the more southern reaches of the area, who made extensive use of copper for tools and implements; they are known to us as the Old Copper Culture people, and are believed to have endured from 5000 B.C. to 1500 B.C. Sites of this culture have been found in numerous places in Wisconsin, Minnesota, and at Reflection Bay, Lake Nipigon, and elsewhere in Ontario. Later cultures were the Early Woodland, which seems to have come to an end between 500 B.C. and 100 B.C.; it was characterized by burial mounds, pottery, and possibly the use of tobacco and the pipe; and the Middle Woodland and Late Woodland cultures which succeeded it. There is much yet to be learned about these, as well as about the earlier cultures, and several students are engaged in the task or have already contributed to it. Dr. R. S. MacNeish of the University of Calgary, Dr. Norman Emerson and Dr. Robert C. Dailey of the University of Toronto, Dr. George I. Quimby of the University of Washington, and Walter A. Kenyon of the Royal Ontario Museum are some of the investigators of the numerous problems which still remain before the prehistory of the Shield country will become clear. (For further reading, consult: Quimby, *Indian Life in the Upper Great Lakes*; MacNeish, *Introduction to the Archaeology of Southeast Manitoba*.)

The break between the archaeological and the ethnological cultures came of course with the arrival on the scene of the first white men. None of the explorers mention, so far as this writer is aware, the presence of pottery among the Indians whom they met in the Shield country, but in most other respects the Indians seem to have been living much as they had been doing for a

The Grassy Narrows scroll

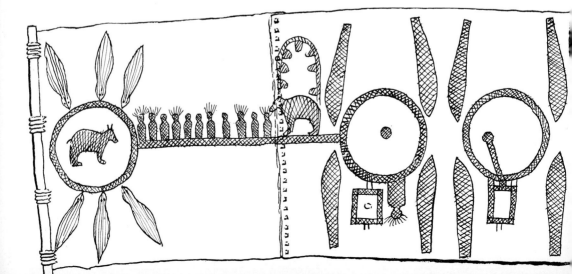

long time. Perhaps pottery was only used in places where it was convenient to do so, although this does not seem to have been the case in prehistoric times. In any event, the historic Indians were all Algonkian-speaking, with the possible exception that there may have been some Siouan-speaking groups west of Lake Superior, and all may be classed in the ethnographic group of Eastern Woodlands people. Precisely where the various Indian groups were living when the country was first visited by white men it is now impossible to say with assurance, but it would appear that the Ottawas and the Nipissings were living east of Georgian Bay and perhaps northward, while the Ojibwa occupied virtually all the remainder of the Ontario portion of the Shield as well as the southern shores of Lake Superior. The Cree lived on parts of the Shield in Quebec, Manitoba, and westward, but probably never held any parts of it in Ontario. It is known that during the historic period there have been various movements of peoples, probably not of great significance so far as rock paintings are concerned, but deserving of note. The Ottawa, after much wandering, finally came to settle chiefly on Manitoulin Island, while the Ojibwa moved into the territory lately vacated by them. The Ojibwa also moved into the southern peninsula of Ontario, which had once been the homeland of the Huron and their kin, and have occupied those portions of the Shield which lie in that part of the Province, as well as some other areas. At the time when this expansion was taking place, a branch of the Ojibwa, living near the falls of St. Mary's River, and for that reason known to the French as the Saulteurs (or Saulteaux), began to push westward over large portions of the present districts of Kenora and Rainy River and even further west. The cultural differences among these groups, however, is slight. One of the most interesting aspects of their life, from the point of view of the present discussion, is the existence among the Ojibwa of the secret society called the Grand Medicine Society or Midaywiwin. This organization was extremely important in Ojibwa life, and most men strove to become members of it at some time during their lifetime. Those who became leaders or Miday were

167

(*see* page 13)

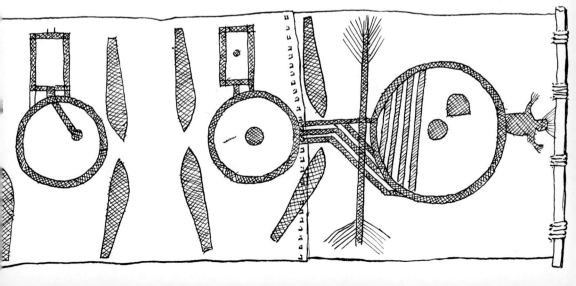

thought to possess great supernatural power; they had long rituals to remember, and to help them to do so they frequently recorded them upon rolls of birchbark. Pictures of birds, animals, and men were scratched into the inner surface of the bark to serve as a reminder of the various stages in the ceremony and of the sequence of songs. It was also rather common for the men to scratch symbols of their clans upon their war clubs, pipe stems, and other personal belongings, and the same symbols were sometimes incised upon their grave markers.

From what has already been said, it is clear that the Indian occupation of the Canadian Shield country goes a long way back in time, and that there has been a succession of peoples living in it. That there was change and movements of groups is certain. The rock paintings could, at least in theory, be due in whole or in part to any one of them. In practice, it seems impossible that any of the paintings could have withstood the severe weathering to which they would have been subjected during the time-span covered by the period of human occupation. To this writer, it seems improbable that they could have lasted even since Early Woodland times. If this reasoning holds, those now in existence are most likely the work of a people of Woodland culture, probably the Late Woodland of prehistoric and Eastern Woodland of early historic times.

The rock paintings in Ontario are drawings of various sorts usually made on the smooth surface of granite or similar rock outcroppings along the shores of lakes and rivers. Vertical or nearly vertical faces presented the most desirable situations, but this could be affected by the presence of lichens, fissures, and so on. Not all smooth rock faces were utilized, nor were all those near streams and lakes; the choice was seemingly capricious but may have depended upon factors at which we can only guess. Even today, miscellaneous little objects seemingly purposely left by Indians at the sites of some rock paintings suggest the idea of offerings to spirits of the place; if this is so, an idea that the place was the abode of spirits may have been one of the controlling factors in the choice of sites. As for lichen-covered rocks, it would seem natural that the Indians would avoid them as locations for their rock paintings, but other considerations may have dictated otherwise. (Lichens have probably destroyed many rock paintings, but how extensive such damage may be it would be impossible to determine. Studies are being made on the growth of lichen, and on other matters connected with them, which may throw some light on the problem.)

It is conceivable that there is some pattern or plan to the general location of rock paintings, but, if this is true, it has still to be worked out. Were they placed only at the abodes of spirits? Were they scattered haphazardly in remote as well as in accessible places? Were they located only along important routes, or along routes used only at certain seasons or for certain purposes? The answers to these, and to many other questions, still have to be found, but should be interesting when discovered.

If a naturally smooth rock face was always chosen, it would not be necessary for the artist to prepare it for painting in any way. He would, however, need to select a face which he could reach from a canoe or at least from the ice; that is, an almost sheer cliff rising from the water. Failing such a site, he could and often did choose a face which, though well above the water level, could still be reached from a ledge. Only a very few rock paintings exist in Ontario where the means of access is not now apparent. Having selected the location, and presumably made whatever religious observances may have been necessary, the Indian painter still needed to make ready his pigments. This was seldom an arduous task, for the Indians were well aware of innumerable sources of pigment and were entirely familiar with their preparation and uses. They employed them extensively in early historic times and almost certainly in prehistoric times as well to paint designs upon their faces, arms, and bodies, and sometimes upon their belongings. Moreover, the pigments used in rock paintings—namely, the two oxides of iron—were abundant in the area, and it was only necessary to gather them and crush them to a powder. A white pigment, whose composition is uncertain, was occasionally used in the rock paintings; it may have been guano, or a white earth. The iron oxides, when mixed with some binder, were ready for use. Although preliminary tests have been made to determine the nature of this binder, it remains unknown. More complicated tests may reveal its identity. At any rate, good binders were certainly available to the Indians, and beyond a doubt they used one or more of them, and possibly all. Gulls' eggs would serve admirably and bears' grease would likewise suffice. Beaver tails and fish roe, the hoofs of moose and deer, could all be boiled to make glue, and fish and rabbit skins may have been utilized also. Any one of these, mixed with red ochre or white earth, would adhere well to the rock. From the examination so far made, it appears that the binder leaches out in time, leaving the pigment firmly attached to the microscopic indentations and convexities of the rock surface. The oxide pigments were of two colours, red and yellow; but since they were seldom pure, all gradations between these may be found in the paintings. The colours were in some cases applied with the fingers, as Dewdney has pointed out on p. 17, but it seems likely that brushes, probably made by breaking back the fibres of small plants like the willow would frequently serve as well. Whether brushes made of moose or deer hair were used is problematical, though they could readily have been made. With such simple equipment— mineral pigments, grease or glue, fingers or a simple brush, and a canoe to stand in when the work was done in the summer—the great panoply of Shield country rock paintings must have been done.

The rock paintings still in existence mirror indirectly some aspects of their makers' attitudes to their external world and something of their thinking. They portray certain of their game animals, such as moose and bear; and the canoes and wigwams shown illustrate the world of their own creation. Over and above these aspects, the paintings also illustrate some of the creatures of the native's mind, in the shape of mythical or supernatural beings like the thunderbird, the serpent, the turtle, and the pipe-smoking moose. All of the pictures were presumably placed on the rocks for some purpose, the most obvious being to convey a message. If they were intended as messages, some were probably addressed to the attention of other Indians; some to the inhabitants of the spirit world. Any which were not, strictly speaking, messages may have been memorials of one sort or another, illustrations of myths, or markers of spots of some ritual or other significance. These are but suggestions of the purposes which may have motivated the placing of the rock paintings where they are found today.

As Dewdney has made clear, they have already yielded much information upon such matters as technique and art styles, and shown that some of the sites were used more than once. There is still much that is not understood, however, and the remaining questions pose a challenge to further study. We should like to know if the rock paintings were all made by the same people; over what time-span they were created; the significance of the various paintings; the meaning of the conventionalized symbols, and many more hidden matters.

Three generations ago, Garrick Mallery wrote that "the interpretation of the ancient forms is to be obtained, if at all, not by the discovery of any hermeneutic key, but by an understanding of the modern forms, some of which fortunately can be interpreted by living men; and when this is not the case the more recent forms can be made intelligible at least in part by a thorough knowledge of the historic tribes, including their sociology, philosophy, and arts, such as is becoming acquired, and of their sign language" (Mallery, 1886, p. 16). What Mallery wrote then still holds today for the Great Lakes rock paintings, except that now it would be extremely difficult to find living men who could reliably interpret any of them. But it seems true that a sound knowledge of Ojibwa—or if one prefers, central Algonkian— mythology, legends, ritual practices, and material culture would go a long way towards elucidating many of the symbols and pictures on the rocks. Perhaps of all these aspects of culture, the myths and legends are the most important, for often supernatural creatures are described in them. Following these, a knowledge of the practices of the Midaywiwin or Grand Medicine Society, with its accompanying mnemonic records on birchbark rolls, would be helpful. Bark records of other sorts could also supply some clues. The sign language may have some utility, as Mallery believed it would, for it was widely used and understood; it should be examined with the interpretation of the rock paintings in mind.

Except in the case of the paintings at Agawa Rock, we have no first-hand interpretation of the meanings. The interpretation of these depends upon copies made by Indians on birchbark for Henry Schoolcraft, and upon the verbal descriptions of them which the Indians gave him. They suggest that each symbol was intended to be read by itself, and the meanings then com-

170

A shaman
in a sweat
lodge?

bined and modified so as to make sense; the four disks over the two convex lines at Agawa Rock are taken to indicate a four days' (or suns') journey over the basin of the water. This is in marked distinction to the bark etchings, in which the figures or symbols are arranged in horizontal lines, and the "reading" or interpretation is intended to begin at the right or left and proceed in either direction. The ideas are thus linked in a sequence. In the rock paintings, it appears that they should be considered as a unit, though there may be more than one unit in a group.

The afore-mentioned bark rolls of the Midaywiwin often afford important clues to the identity of the symbols in the rocks. Several of them, for example, show tree-like figures which are interpreted as the "tree of medicine." A similar figure appears in Face IX at Site 7, along with a conventionalized figure of a man inside a wigwam-like structure. From a knowledge of Ojibwa

171

culture it is possible to conjecture that this group was intended to show a shaman taking a sweat bath in a sweat lodge (which is constructed like a miniature wigwam), for this ceremony of physical and spiritual purification had to be gone through before he could undertake an important ritual, and that he would then use some of the "tree of medicine." Or again, one finds in the Miday rolls figures of birds, some of which are described as such powerful creatures as the grey eagle, others as the thunderbird. Both may be shown naturalistically or conventionally. Similar figures occur on the rock paintings, though the conventionalized form seems to be more common, and the assumption, perhaps not warranted in all cases, is that the thunderbird is meant. Unlike the eagle, the thunderbird was a supernatural creature who lived high in the sky beyond the sight of men, but made his presence known by flapping his wings to cause the thunder, and by blinking his eyes to cause the lightning. Still a third symbol in the rock paintings may be identified by means of the bark rolls, and this is the Great Lynx or Mishipizhiw. Mishipizhiw is also a supernatural creature, highly dangerous, who inhabits the rapids on some streams; for instance, the Manitou Rapids on the Rainy River, near Emo. He appears in some of the bark rolls as a cat-like creature with large ears or horns and a long tail. So frequent a motif did he become in Ojibwa art that he is sometimes depicted on their woven bags. Mishipizhiw undoubtedly appears at Site 36 in the normal form. John Tanner (James, *A Narrative of the Captivity . . . of John Tanner*, p. 335), an early author who lived most of his life among the Ojibwa, illustrated the Great Lynx as a cat-like creature with spiny back, and from this and similar evidence, we may assume that the spiny-backed creature which looks like a horned serpent at Site 8 is also intended for him. It is worthy of note here that in the bark rolls, lines radiating from a figure of a man or an animal are meant to imply "power" in that figure; hence the spines on the back of the Great Lynx may be a device for emphasizing his great supernatural power.

By comparing the pictures in the rock paintings one by one with those on

172

Human
figure
from
Blindfold
Lake
site

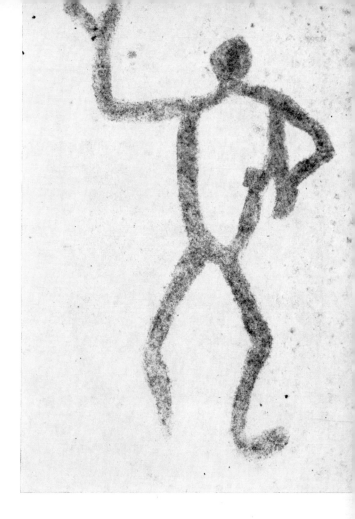

the birchbark rolls and other records referring to the Algonkians of the Great Lakes area, it should be possible to identify many more of them. A similar study of the supernatural beings in the mythology of the Algonkians is likely to result in further identifications.

Even though the identity of one or more symbols or figures in a rock painting may have been established, the signification of the group as a whole may still remain to be solved. It is not, apparently, a simple procedure of adding one identification to another and getting a sort of sentence as a result. Alternative meanings may be possible for one or more of the figures, and it then becomes a matter of choosing between the alternatives until one has hit upon a combination which makes sense. Of course, in some cases, the meaning may be fairly obvious, but in others the solution may be extremely difficult.

Even the Miday bark rolls, although the commonest of Ojibwa records and the most generally understood, are said to be sometimes quite beyond the comprehension of Ojibwa men who have not seen that particular roll before, as has been already noted. Likewise, the rock paintings—even the most recent—may present difficulties in total interpretation which defy solution.

It is thus possible to compare the rock paintings in the Shield country with the drawings to be seen in the Miday rolls and other incised bark and wood records, and with the descriptions to be found in the myths and legends of the historic occupants. By the same token, they may be compared with rock paintings and other pictorial representations from other areas, and with the descriptions in non-Algonkian mythologies and similar sources. It should also be borne in mind that some of the Algonkian legends and myths may be based upon rock paintings from an earlier, pre-Algonkian occupation of the country, in which case the lines of distinction might be considerably blurred. This does not rule out the possibility, however, that some of the rock paintings, if they antedate the Algonkian occupation, may have only a superficial connection with that occupation; indeed, they might well reflect a quite different set of ideas and a different galaxy of supernatural beings and be executed in a different style.

Such differences in style might be demonstrated by one or other of the techniques described by Dewdney, and by the rather mechanical process of putting each recorded symbol or figure on an index card. The cards might then be sorted and the various symbols grouped together in such a way that there was a progression by minor changes from a more obvious or naturalistic form (e.g. a moose) to a conventional or abstract form. A procedure of this sort might help to identify some symbols not now understood, but, perhaps more important, it might be able to reveal whether there is a residue of symbols which cannot be connected stylistically with others. If there are figures or symbols which cannot be shown to be related to any of those connected with Ojibwa life, there would be a presumption that they might be attributable to people of another culture. Whether such a culture were earlier than the Algonkian occupation would have to be proven by some acceptable method of dating still to be devised.

After several seasons' work, a good representation of the kind of rock paintings left by the Indians of the Great Lakes has been recorded, and is now available for study. It will serve, if no more should be collected, to illustrate the condition, variety, and geographical range of this manifestation of aboriginal occupation of the Canadian Shield. As a form of expression the rock paintings are interesting in themselves. But over and above this, they illuminate some aspects of aboriginal life and culture. Further analysis should yield some clues as to movements of people within the area, and may throw some light upon beliefs held by those groups. Even though much of the information they hold may remain forever hidden from us, the search for it is always alluring, and each clue found is worthy of the effort.

174

Epilogue

Ten years have now passed since we began the pictograph recording programme in the Great Lakes area. For the field recorder, this has meant numerous trips into many remote parts; trips by land, water, by air, and combinations of all three; delays, hardships, and frustrations; encounters with black flies and mosquitoes; plenty of hard and sometimes dangerous work. On the other hand, it has meant many pleasant experiences in this quite delightful part of Canada and the neighbouring United States, and a chance to enjoy beauty and tranquillity.

For the rest of us and for posterity, it has meant the gathering of a wealth of information about rock paintings in this vast area, including many drawings and reproductions. Dewdney has recorded one hundred and fifty-two such sites in Ontario alone. He has made over one thousand colour transparencies, prepared scale drawings of every site, and painted forty-seven full-size watercolour reproductions of individual pictographs. No one else in Canada has visited and recorded so many rock art sites, collected so much field data upon them and and their occurrences, nor studied so intensively so large an area.

When the programme was begun, it was hardly dreamed that the results would be of such magnitude. It was, in fact, anticipated that the rock paintings would be found more or less evenly distributed throughout the entire Quetico-Superior woodlands, and that they would be reported by interested individuals from time to time. In actual fact, the search was bolstered—and speeded up— not only by Dewdney's enthusiasm and diligence, but by the interest taken by the personnel of the Department of Lands and Forests, camp operators and outfitters, and interested people of the area generally.

Despite the highly gratifying results, we should state that the last site has not been found. Almost certainly, new ones will come to light from time to time in the years to come. We can be reasonably confident, however, that the largest proportion of our rock art sites has now been seen and recorded, and that very few, if any, really important ones still remain to be discovered. From those we know, we may fairly conclude that rock art was not practised uniformly throughout the area, but was, quite assiduously, in the western part.

Regarded strictly as a recording project, the programme has been quite successful and, as such, is of national importance. It has added—or rather, rescued from oblivion—a most interesting phase of aboriginal activity, one which would otherwise have been lost through natural agencies and with the settlement of the country. It has added an art form of considerable interest to the repertoire of truly Canadian culture; a form which has already begun to inspire new, creative work, and which we hope will continue to inspire Canadian artists in the future. There is every indication that this encouraging development is soundly based.

Equally important and significant are the opportunities which the collected data will afford for scientific and historical analysis. First among these—and perhaps the most manageable—is the study of rock painting distribution. We already know that the sites occur predominantly in the western portions of the Great Lakes region, scattering and thinning out towards the northern edge of the Shield. Further study may narrow still further the places of concentration. The question naturally arises: why should such concentrations exist? Is it a purely cultural phenomenon, or is it in some way related to the nature of the environment? Only an intensive study of the art forms from each site, combined with an equally intensive examination of the nature of all sites, will reveal the answer.

Dewdney has already suggested the existence of more than one art style, and no doubt the more recent records will allow refinements on the first conclusions to be made. It may well be that in some areas there has been a sequence of styles; in others it may be possible to demonstrate that a single style originated, or prevailed, in one area and spread thence to others, perhaps overwhelming earlier manifestations. And, if it can be unequivocally demonstrated that different styles exist, what is the explanation? Do the earlier indicate the presence of a different people from those who painted the later pictures; different, that is, culturally and possibly physically? Or does it imply some sort of shift in religious attitudes and cosmological outlook? These are challenging problems to which the records may hold clues.

With new knowledge gained from the study of the Great Lakes pictographs, it is tempting to move on to compare them with similar rock pictures from adjacent regions to the east, west, north, and south. As it happens, there has been a resurgence of interest in rock art in recent years, stimulated in part, at least in North America, by the construction of great irrigation dams and the necessary submergence of large areas where such forms occur, so that the body of information on them is now considerably greater than two decades ago. It should thus be possible to compare those of one region with those of another; it is likely that adjacent regions will show many characters in common, and those widely separated, unique ones. Regional styles may therefore be identified and the study put on a scientific base. Such extended studies may yield clues to areal cultural sequences and possibly in some cases provide evidence for migrations.

As already suggested, it is now extremely difficult to decipher the meaning of most of the rock paintings. Conceivably, it might be possible to do so with computers, but this does not look too promising at present because the episodes or situations depicted were likely to be of a highly personal nature. Even to guess would require that we undergo the same experiences as the artists—an obvious impossibility. Some of the pictures are sufficiently stereotyped and stylized to be recognizable, as the thunderbird, but the significance of many will, presumably, remain inscrutable.

Nevertheless, the field and museum research have been well worth the time, effort, and expense. Compared to archaeological investigation and analysis in other countries, studies of our rock paintings are still in their infancy. It is gratifying that so much has been, in a sense, salvaged, and then recorded in so short a time. These have been the important functions to date. While it is true that definitive analysis and interpretations may still elude us at this time, we do know that our investigations have provided us with a distinctive, if intriguing, form of indigenous art that already has given inspiration to Canadian artists in this second half of the twentieth century.

Photograph by J. M. Vanderleek

Smirch Lake

Acknowledgments

IN ADDITION to the general and special acknowledgements made herein Mr. Dewdney is anxious to record the following:

"Above all I should like to record the invaluable aid in tracking down ethnological clues furnished by the late Chief James Horton of Manitou Rapids. A gentle man of unfailing courtesy and unpretentious dignity, greatly gifted as a teller of Ojibwa tales, his death was an incalculable loss. Of other Ojibwa who generously shared with me the lore of their forefathers, I should particularly like to mention Messrs. Norval Morriseau and Thomas Paishk of Red Lake, Mr. Jack Bushy of Ignace, and Mr. Charles Friday of Seine River. I am also especially indebted to Dr. C. L. Hannay of London, Ontario, whose superb photographs of the Grassy Narrows scroll made it possible for me to reproduce it in accurate detail.

"To the many other friends who have cheerfully provided hospitality, transportation, clues, directions, and helpful information, both in the field and by correspondence, my personal thanks. Without the help of each, this book would have been the poorer."

MR. KIDD wishes especially to thank Dr. and Mrs. E. S. Rogers for making numerous suggestions concerning his manuscript.

Dr. V. B. Meen also read the manuscript and offered helpful advice.

Appendixes

Bibliography

ARCHAEOLOGICAL REPORTS, Appendix to the Report of the Minister of Education (Ontario) for the years 1893–4, by David Boyle, *Rock Paintings, or Petrographs, Rock Paintings at Lake Massanog* (Lake Mazinaw); 1904, *Picture Writing*; 1906, *Rock Paintings at Timagami District* (Lady Evelyn and Diamond Lakes); 1907, *Rock Paintings* (mouth of Nipigon River).

BEAUGRAND, H., *New Studies of Canadian Folklore* (Montreal, 1904).

BESCHEL, ROLAND E., "Dating Rock Surfaces by Lichen Growth and Its Application to Glaciology and Physiography (Lichenometry)," in G. O. Raasch (ed.), *Geology of the Arctic*, II (Toronto, 1961).

BLESSING, FRED K., "Birchbark Mide Scrolls from Minnesota," *Minnesota Archeologist*, July, 1963.

BOAS, FRANZ, *Primitive Art* (New York, 1955).

BRAY, WILLIAM, "Observations on the Indian method of picture-writing by William Bray, Esq., in a letter to the Secretary read March 1, 1781," *Archaeologia*, VI, 1782, 159–62.

BREUIL, ABBÉ HENRI, *The White Lady of the Brandberg* (New York, 1955).

BRINTON, DANIEL G., *The Lenâpe and their legends; with the complete text and symbols of the Walum Olum, a new translation, and an inquiry into its authenticity* (Philadelphia, 1885).

CHERNETSOV, VALERY N., *Naskalnye Izobrazheniya Urala* (Moscow, 1964).

CHRISTENSEN, ERWIN O., *Primitive Art* (New York, 1955).

COATSWORTH, EMERSON S., *The Indians of Quetico* (Toronto, 1957).

COPWAY, GEORGE, *The Traditional History and Characteristic Sketches of the Ojibway Nation* (Boston, 1851).

DELAFIELD, MAJOR JOSEPH, *The Unfortified Boundary* (New York, 1843).

DENSMORE, FRANCES, *Chippewa Music*, 2 Vols. (Washington, 1910–13).

DEWDNEY, SELWYN, "Stone-age art in the Canadian Shield," *Canadian Art*, XVI (3), 1959, 164–7.

———— "The Quetico Pictographs," *The Beaver* (Hudson's Bay Company, Winnipeg), Summer 1958, 15–22.

———— "Indian Rock Art," Popular Series 4, Saskatchewan Museum of Natural History (Regina, 1963).

———— "Writings on Stone Along the Milk River," *The Beaver*, Winter, 1964.

———— "Stone Age Paintings," Heritage Area Publication, Manitoba Department of Mines (Winnipeg, 1965).

GEIDION, S., *The Beginnings of Art* (Washington, 1962).

GRANT, CAMPBELL, *The Rock Paintings of the Chumash* (Berkeley, 1965).

HALLOWELL, A. Irving, "The Role of Conjuring in Saulteaux Society," *Publications*

180

of the Philadelphia Anthropological Society, II (Philadelphia, 1942).

HEIZER, R. F. and SAUMHOFF, M. A., *Prehistoric Rock Art of Nevada and Eastern California* (Berkeley, 1962).

HEWITT, J. N. B., and WILLIAM N. FENTON, "Some mnemonic pictographs relating to the Iroquois Condolence Council," *Journal of the Washington Academy of Sciences*, 35 (10), Oct. 15, 1945.

HOFFMAN, W. J., "Pictography and shamanistic rites of the Ojibwa," *American Anthropologist*, ser. 1, I, 1888, 209–29.

——— "The Midéwiwin or 'Grand Medicine Society' of the Ojibwa," Smithsonian Institution, Bureau of American Ethnology, *7th Annual Report*, 1891 (1892) (Washington, D.C., 1892).

JACKSON, A. T., "Picture-writing of Texas Indians," *University of Texas Publication no. 3809*, Anthropological Papers, II, 1938.

JAMES, EDWIN (ed.), *A Narrative of the Captivity and Adventures of John Tanner* . . . (New York, 1830; Minneapolis, 1956).

JOHNSON, TOWNLEY, "Facsimile tracing and redrawing of rock-paintings," *South African Archaeological Bulletin*, XIII (50), 1958, 67–9.

KEESING, FELIX M., "The Menomini Indians of Wisconsin. A study of three centuries of cultural contact and change," *American Philosophical Society*, memoirs X, 1939.

KINIETZ, W. VERNON, "Birch bark records among the Chippewa," *Indiana Academy of Science, Proceedings*, XLIX, 1939, 38–40.

——— "The Indians of the western great lakes, 1615–1760," *Occasional Contributions from the Museum of Anthropology* (University of Michigan), X, 1940. See under *Chippewa*, 317–29.

KOHL, JOHANN, G., *Kitchi-gami* (trans. from German, London, 1860; with Introduction by R. W. Fridley, Minneapolis, 1956).

LAMING, ANNETTE, *Lascaux Paintings and Engravings* (Baltimore, 1959).

LEE, THOMAS E., "The second Sheguiandah expedition, Manitoulin Island, Ontario," *American Antiquity*, XXI(1), 1955, 63–71.

LEECHMAN, DOUGLAS, "Some pictographs of southeastern British Columbia," *Transactions of the Royal Society of Canada*, 3rd ser, XLVIII, Sec. II, 1954, 77–85.

LEECHMAN, DOUGLAS, *et al.*, "Pictographs in Southwestern Alberta," *Annual Report* (National Museum, Ottawa), 1953–4.

LHOTE, HENRI, *The Search for the Tassili Frescoes* (translated by A. H. Brodrick Hutchinson, London, 1959).

LYFORD, CARRIE A., "Ojibwa crafts (Chippewa)," *Indian Handcrafts*, V (Lawrence, Kansas, 1953).

MCCARTHY, F. D., *Australian Aboriginal Rock Art* (Sidney, 1962).

MACFIE, JOHN A., "The stories on the cliffs," *Sylva*, XV(6), 1959, 17–20.

MACNEISH, RICHARD S., "An introduction to the archaeology of southeast Manitoba," *National Museum of Canada, Bulletin 157* (Ottawa, 1958).

MALLERY, GARRICK, "Pictographs of the North American Indians: a preliminary paper," Smithsonian Institution, Bureau of American Ethnology, *4th Annual Report*, 1886, 3–256 (Washington, D.C., 1887).

——— "Picture-writing of the American Indians," *ibid.*, *10th Annual Report*, 1893, 3–807 (Washington, D.C., 1894).

——— "Sign language among the North American Indians compared with that among other peoples and deaf-mutes," *ibid., 1st Annual Report*, 1879–1880, 263–552 (Washington, D.C., 1881).

MORRISEAU, NORVAL, *Legends of My People the Great Ojibway*, edited and with an introduction by Selwyn Dewdney (Toronto, 1965).

MURDOCK, GEORGE P., *Ethnographic Bibliography of North America* (New Haven, 1960).

NELSON, N. C., "South African rock pictures," *American Museum of Natural History, Guide Leaflet Series*, 93, 1937.

OKLADNIKOV, A. P., *Shishkinskie Pisanitsy*. Pamyatnik Drevney Kultury Pribaikalia (Irkutskoe Knizhnoe Izdatelstvo, 1959).

——— *Naskalnye Risunki*, Kamienykh Ostrovov (Irkutsk, 1960).

OLSON, SIGURD F., "Painted rocks," *National Parks Magazine* (Washington), XXXV (163), 1961, 4–7.

QUIMBY, GEORGE I., "New evidence links Chippewa to prehistoric cultures," *Chicago Natural History Museum Bulletin*, XXIX (1), 1958, 7–8.

——— *Indian life in the Upper Great Lakes, 11,000 B.C. to A.D. 1800* (Chicago, 1960).

RADIN, PAUL, and A. B. REAGAN, "Ojibwa myths and tales," *Journal of American Folklore*, XLI, 1928, 61–146.

SAUNDERS, R. M., "The first introduction of European plants and animals into Canada," *Canadian Historical Review*, XVI(4), 1935, 388–406.

SCHOOLCRAFT, HENRY, *The American Indians* (Rochester, 1851).

SMITH, HARLAN I., An Album of Prehistoric Canadian Art, *Canadian Dept. of Mines Bulletin #37* (Victoria Memorial Museum Anthropological #8, 1923).

SOMMERS, ROGER, *Prehistoric rock art of the Federation of Rhodesia & Nyasaland*: Paintings and descriptions by Elizabeth Goodall, C. K. Cooke [and] J. Desmond Clark (Salisbury, 1959).

SPECK, FRANK G., "Montagnais Art in Birchbark: A Circumpolar Trait," *Indian Notes and Monographs*, XI (2) (New York, 1937).

SWAUGER, JAMES L., "Petroglyphs at the Hamilton Farm Site," *West Virginia Archeologist* (15), February, 1963.

SWEETMAN, PAUL W., "A preliminary report on the Peterborough petroglyphs," *Ontario History*, xlvii (3), 1955.

VOEGELIN, ERMINIE W., "Notes on Ojibwa—Ottawa pictography," *Indiana Academy of Science, Proceedings*, LI, 1941, 44–7.

WARREN, WILLIAM W., "History of the Ojibways, based upon tradition and oral statements," *Minnesota Historical Collections*, V, 1885.

WINCHELL, NEWTON H., *The Aborigines of Minnesota* . . . (St. Paul, 1911).

WINDELS, FERNAND, *The Lascaux Cave Paintings* (New York, 1950).

Pictograph Sites

SITES marked by (*) are not illustrated in this book. Sites marked by (†) are outside of the Canadian Shield.

1957

1. Agnes Lake, south of Narrows, Quetico Provincial Park, 25, 26
2. Agnes Lake, centre, Q.P.P., 27, 60
3. "Ahsin Lake," southwest of Williams Lake, Q.P.P., 26
4. *"Keewatin Lake," between Agnes and Kawnipi, Q.P.P., 26
5. Lac la Croix, Irving Island, Q.P.P., 3, 26–31, 84
6. *Lac la Croix, just west of site # 5, Q.P.P.
7. Crooked Lake, Basswood River, Minn., 16, 31–32, 115
8. Darky Lake, Q.P.P., 35, 36, 38, 42, 172
9. *Burt Lake, Q.P.P., 36
10. An unnamed lake north of Hurlburt Lake, Q.P.P., 36
11. *Agnes Lake, central west shore, Q.P.P., 36

1958

12. Cache Bay, Q.P.P., 16, 32, 34, 36, 42
13. Northern Lights Lake, Nelson Bay
14. Northern Lights Lake, Trafalgar Bay, 34
15. Pictured Lake, southwest of Fort William, 56, 75, 76
16. Hegman Lake, Superior National Forest, Minnesota, 16, 38, 40
17. Kawishiwi River, south of Lake Alice, S.N.F., Minn, 39
18. Burntside Lake, west of Ely, Minn., 39, 75
19. *Island River, south of Isabella Lake, S.N.F., Minn., 38, 39
20. *Nett Lake, Minnesota (petroglyphs), 36, 40, 44
21. Lower Manitou Lake, west shore of Narrows, 73, 74
22. Painted Narrows, Rainy Lake, 16, 42, 91
23. Namakan Narrows, north entrance, 40, 41
24. Namakan Narrows, centre, 40, 41
25. Namakan Lake, island in east end, 40, 41
26. Cuttle Lake, small site, 71, 72
27. Cuttle Lake, large site, 10, 11, 71, 72, 73
28. Southwest of Sioux Narrows, Lake of the Woods, 48, 50, 51
29. Blindfold Lake, 2, 48, 57
30. *"Irene Lake," east of Kenora
31. Northern Twin Lake, 4–7
32. *Orient Bay, south of Royal Windsor Lodge, 77, 78
33. *French River, east of Recollect Falls, 95
34. Ninth Lake, East Spanish River, 90, 91
35. Fairy Point, Lake Missinaibi, 2, 86–89
36. Agawa Rock, Lake Superior Provincial Park, 10, 14, 16, 17, 81–83, 148, 149, 171, 172

1959

37. Mazinaw Lake, Bon Echo Provincial Park, 24, 96–102
38. Little Mazinaw Lake, south of Bon Echo, 96, 97, 102
39. Collins Inlet, Georgian Bay, 94

144. Donnelly River (II), 113
145. Deer Lake, McIntosh Bay, 114
146. Hanging Lake, 114
147. Roderick Lake (I), 115
148. Roderick Lake (II), 115
149. Pine Needle Lake (I), 122, 123

1963

150. Horwood Lake, Hardiman Bay, 150, 151
151. Harmon Lake, 133
152. Kitchiwatchi Lake, 133
153. Pine Needle Lake (II), 123
154. Bloodvein River, east of Larus Lake, 118, 119
155. Abamatagwia Lake, 129, 130
156. Lac la Croix, Beatty Portage, 106, 107
157. Darky Lake (II), 105
158. Kahshahpiwi Lake, 106
   (Sites numbered 159 to 185, inclusive, were recorded in Alberta, Saskatchewan, and Manitoba.)
186. Dryberry Lake (III), 125
187. *Rush Bay (petroglyphs), 110
188. *White Partridge Bay, Lake of the Woods (petroglyphs), 110
189. Teggau Lake (I), 126, 127
190. Teggau Lake (II), 126, 127

1964

191. Brockville, 157
192. Brockville Narrows, 158
193. Barbara Lake, 141, 142
194. Kaiashkomin Lake, 128
195. Jackfish Lake, 108, 109
196. Burditt Lake, 108
197. Sabaskong Bay (I), 110
198. Sabaskong Bay (II), 110
   (Sites numbered 199 to 205, inclusive, were recorded in Saskatchewan and Manitoba.)
206. Sharpstone Lake (II), 115
207. Musclow Lake, 121
208. Frances Lake, 116, 117
209. West of Herod Lake, 115

(Site # 210 was recorded in Manitoba.)
211. Artery Lake, North Arm, 121
212. West of Barclay Lake, 121
213. Bigshell Lake, 121
214. Beamish Lake, 121
215. Hansen Lake, 120, 121
216. *Whitefish Lake (petroglyphs), 134

1965

217. Stony Lake, Nephton ("Peterborough Petroglyphs"), 158
218. Matagamasi Lake, 153
219. Cliff Lake, Mud River (I), 138
220. Cliff Lake, Mud River (II), 138
221. Cliff Lake, Mud River (III), 138
222. Basket Lake, 129
223. White Otter Lake, Ann Bay, 130
224. Silver Lake (I), 110, 111
225. Silver Lake (II), 111
226. Kennedy Island, Lake of the Woods (petroglyphs), 110
227. Kennedy Island (II) (petroglyphs), 110
228. Obabikon Lake, Lake of the Woods, 110
   (Sites 229 to 243, inclusive, were recorded in the NWT, Saskatchewan, and Manitoba.)
244. Lake Matachewan, 152
245. *Severn River, Nighthawk Rapids (lichen glyph), 112, 113
246. Sachigo River, 112
247. *Osnaburgh, Lake St. Joseph, 124
248. Bluffy Lake, 123, 124
249. Lac des Iles, 134

1966

(Sites numbered 250 to 259, inclusive, were recorded in Manitoba.)
260. Rainy Lake, Crowrock Inlet, 107
261. Kawnipi Lake, Quetico Park, 106
262. Cliff Lake, Mud River, 138, 139
263. Cliff Lake, Mud River, 140
264. Cliff Lake, Mud River, 141

Index

187

188